Mehr Erfolg in Englisch

5. Klasse

Grammatik und Wortschatz

Rainer Iwen

Mit ausführlichem Lösungsteil

In Zusammenarbeit mit Langenscheidt

mentor
Eine Klasse besser.

Über den Autor:

Rainer Iwen, Oberstudienrat, Realschulrektor und Studienleiter für Englisch am Institut für Praxis und Theorie der Schule (Landesinstitut für Lehrerfortbildung)

Illustrationen:
Jutta Bauer, Christiane Hansen, Vivien Thiessen, alle Hamburg

Redaktion:
Geraldine Tahmassebi, Elke Spitznagel

Layout:
Sabine Nasko, München

Umschlag:
DESIGN IM KONTOR – Iris Steiner, München

www.mentor.de

Umwelthinweis: Gedruckt auf chlorfrei gebleichtem Papier.

Satz: Franzis print & media GmbH, München
Druck: Mercedes-Druck, Berlin
Bindung: Stein + Lehmann, Berlin
Printed in Germany
ISBN 978-3-580-65540-2

10010

Inhalt

Willkommen!

Hallo, liebe Schülerin, lieber Schüler,

du willst etwas für bessere Noten in Englisch tun?
Gratuliere – den ersten Schritt hast du damit schon geschafft!

Bei den weiteren Schritten wird dich diese Lernhilfe von mentor unterstützen: Du findest hier alle wichtigen **Grammatikregeln** und **Vokabeln,** dazu viele abwechslungsreiche **Übungen**, die wirklich Spaß machen. Und du lernst den lustigen **Fred** kennen, der dir dabei helfen wird.

Du kannst das Buch als Wiederholungskurs von vorne bis hinten durcharbeiten, du kannst aber auch einzelne Kapitel auswählen, die du in der Schule gerade brauchst. Ganz wie du willst! Du kannst mit diesem Buch nämlich ganz alleine arbeiten, ohne Stress.

Besorge dir gleich
- ein paar bunte Stifte zum Anstreichen und Ausmalen,
- ein Extraheft für längere Übungen,
- Bleistift und Radiergummi zum Verbessern.

Die **Lösungen** zu den Übungen findest du hinten im Buch. Aber nicht spicken! Versuche es erst selbst, bevor du nachschaust. Am meisten lernst du, wenn du deine Fehler sorgfältig verbesserst und überlegst, warum du sie gemacht hast.

Wir wünschen dir ganz viel Erfolg in der 5. Klasse!

Rainer Iwen und der mentor Verlag

PS: Wenn dir dieses Buch gefallen hat, würden wir uns riesig freuen, dich in den nächsten Bänden wiederzusehen!

So funktioniert's!

Grammar

In diesen blauen Kästen stehen wichtige Erklärungen zur **Grammatik**, die du meist schon aus der Schule kennst. Lerne bzw. wiederhole sie sorgfältig, denn die brauchst du wirklich!

Words

Hier sind **Vokabeln** übersichtlich zusammengestellt: Auch die solltest du beherrschen!

Info

Hier gibt es weitere **Informationen** zu verschiedenen Themen.

Reading

Hier findest du spannende, lustige, interessante Geschichten, Gedichte oder andere Texte zum **Lesen**. Du wirst staunen, was du schon alles auf Englisch versteht! Und es macht gar nichts aus, wenn du noch nicht alle Wörter kennst.

Dialogue

Hier geht's ums **Sprechen**: Präge dir diese Ausdrücke und Redewendungen gut ein und trau dich, sie bei der nächsten Gelegenheit in der Schule oder außerhalb anzuwenden!

!

Hier heißt es **„Aufgepasst!"**, denn wir geben dir einen Tipp oder weisen dich auf einen Stolperstein hin.

Und ich bin **Fred,** ich helfe dir – versprochen!

1. The Indefinite Article/ Der unbestimmte Artikel

Verwendung und Aussprache

a — a girl, a school, a boy, a new cassette, a unit

a girl a school a boy a new cassette a unit	ein eine	} a	**Aussprache** [ə]

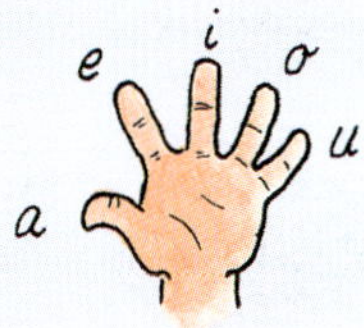

Nur vor Wörtern, die mit einem gesprochenen Vokal (Selbstlaut) anfangen, wird ein **-n** angehängt.

an — an English girl, an old school, an exercise book, an Indian, an apple

an English girl an old school an exercise book an Indian an apple	ein eine	} an	**Aussprache** [ən] vor a, e, i, o, u

Grammar

Manche Wörter – z. B. *unit* [junit] oder *uniform* [ju:niform] – werden zwar am Anfang mit einem Vokal geschrieben, gesprochen wird aber ein Konsonant [ju]. Das heißt, der Artikel ist **a**: ***a unit*** / ***a uniform***

!

1.1 a / an?

Complete the sentences.

1. This is an .... apple.  1. I have got an .... old apple.

2. This is .... orange.  2. I .... big orange.

3. .... American.  3. I .... American book.

4. .... elephant.  4. I .... toy elephant.

5. .... umbrella.  5. I .... small umbrella.

6. .... book.  6. I .... old book.

7. .... uniform.  7. I .... nice uniform.

1.2 Liza's schoolbag

There are lot of things in Liza's schoolbag. Fill in a / an.

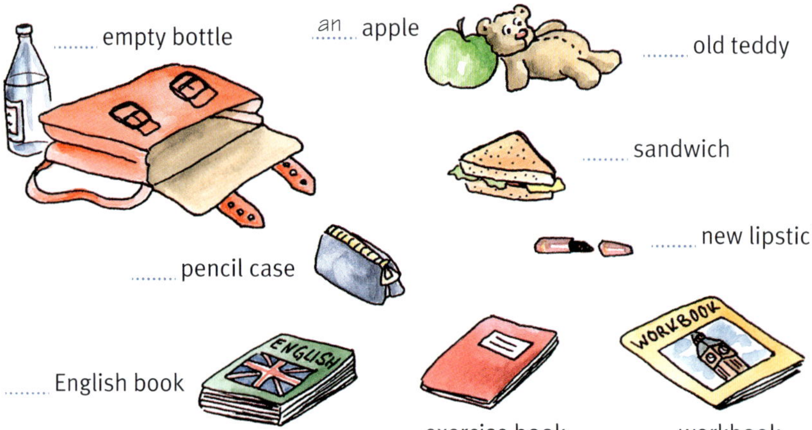

.... empty bottle

an apple

.... old teddy

.... sandwich

.... new lipstick

.... pencil case

.... English book

.... exercise book

.... workbook

1.3 a or an?

Schreib die richtigen Nummern neben die Wörter und sortiere diese in die beiden Kästen unten.

Have a look at the picture and write the numbers of the things in the boxes next to the words.

boy ☐
egg ☐
mouth ☐
tree [1]
car ☐
ear ☐
apple ☐
hand ☐
Englishman ☐
helicopter ☐

eye ☐ house ☐ orange ☐

train ☐ clock ☐ ice cream ☐ idea ☐ girl ☐

a	an
a hand	an ice cream

2. School Things

2.1 Illustrated vocabulary

Words

Write the words under the pictures and read aloud.

pen

felt Lip

ruler

Pencil

~~bag~~ schoolbag

pencil case

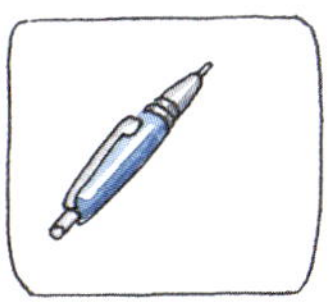

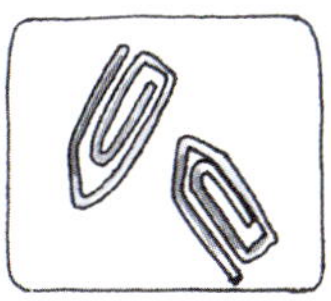

a rubber

glue

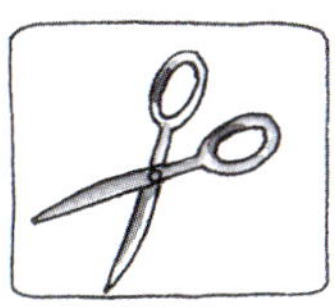

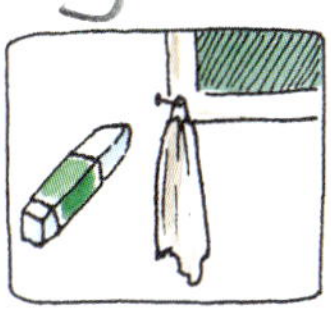

an atlas / sheets of paper / a satchel / a schoolbag / a pencil case / a ruler / paperclips / felt-tip pens / glue / chalk and duster / a dictionary / scissors / a rubber (eraser) / pencils / a globe / coloured pencils / a textbook / a folder / a picture / a biro / a pen / a calculator

2.2 Strange things

Kannst du die Buchstaben in die richtige Reihenfolge bringen?

Can you write the letters in the correct order?

1. koobtxte ... textbook
2. relur ... ruler
3. cipeln ... pencil
4. pne ... pen
5. broi ...
6. scahtle ...
7. ubebrr ... rubber
8. cipeln rephsaren ... pencil sha pena
9. plince sace ... pencil case

2.3 A schoolbag

What's in the bag?

1. pencil 2. ...... 3. ...... 4. ...... 5. ......

6. ...... 7. ...... 8. ...... 9. ......

2.4 A puzzle

Trenne erst die Wörter, dann trage den Satz ein.

Solve the puzzle, then write down the sentence.

Inmybagisagreenpencilcasearulerawhiterubberatextbookaredfeltippenabluepencilasharpenerapadayellowpenandanexercisebook.

In my bag ...

......

......

......

......

......

2.5 A mindmap

Fill in.

Du kannst dir Vokabeln besonders gut merken, wenn du sie dir als Wortnetze aufzeichnest. Diese nennt man auf Englisch *mindmaps*.

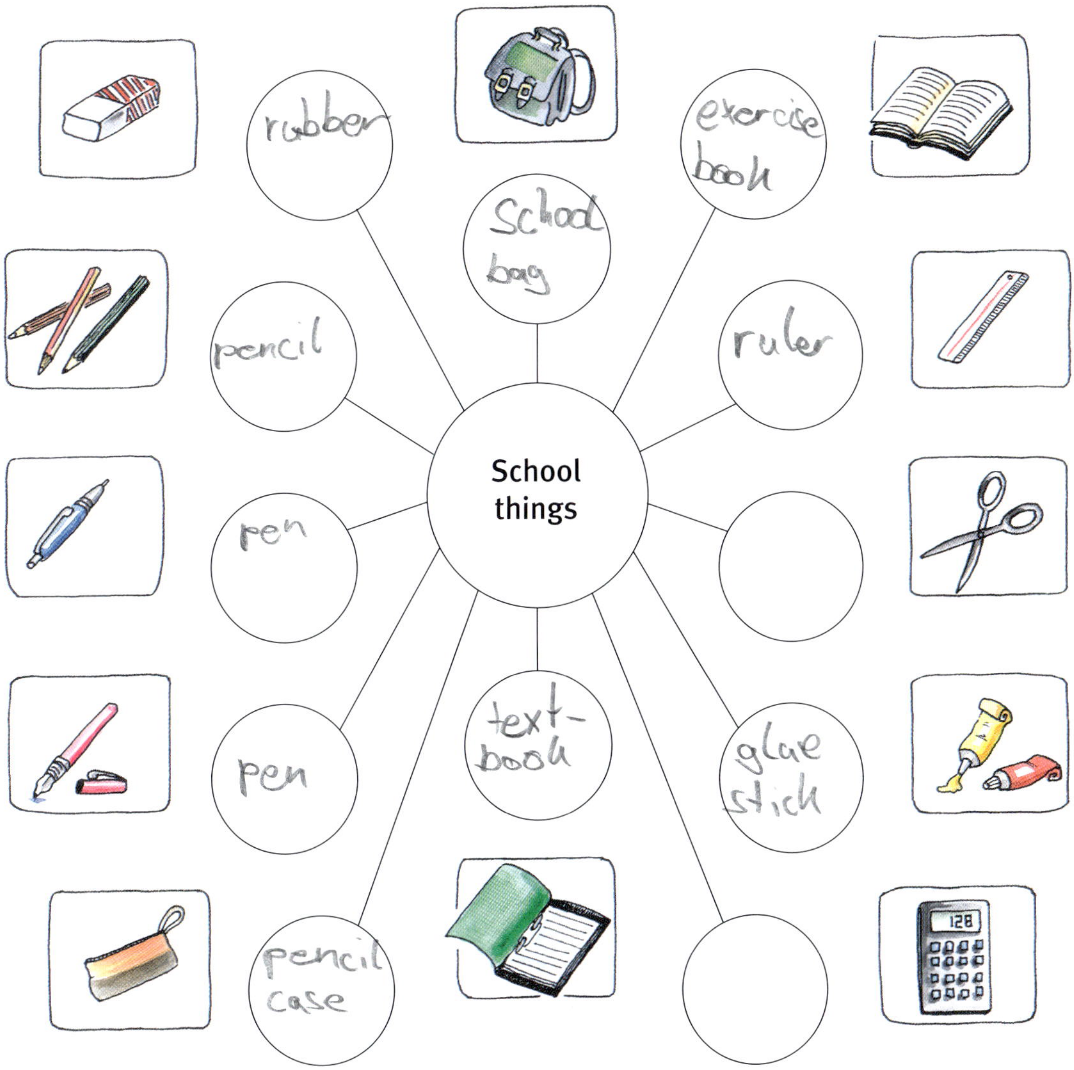

2.6 Over to you: What have you got in your schoolbag?

Look into your schoolbag and write down what you have got and how many.

Reading 2.7 **Getting ready for school – a picture story**

Erzähle die Geschichte. Schreibe die fehlenden Wörter in die Lücken.

Retell the story. Fill in the gaps.

Early in the .... Billy gets up and goes to his ....

He puts a ...., an .... and a geography book into his .... Then he takes his .... and runs out of the .... to go to .... His .... is standing at the .... and tells him that there is no .... today because it is ....

3. In the Classroom

Words

board (1)
light (2)
schoolbag (3)
map (4)
desk (5)
teacher (6)
ruler (7)
Fred (8)
chair (9)
cupboard (10)
book (11)
pen (12)
pupil (13)
rubber (eraser) (14)
chalk (15)
duster (16)

3.1 What is it?

Find the answers.

1. It's in a school and has four walls, a door and a window. — It's a classroom. ....
2. A boy or a girl who goes to school. ....
3. You write with it. ....
4. The teacher writes on it. ....
5. You put books in it in the classroom. ....
6. You sit on it in the classroom. ....
7. It shows countries and hangs on the wall. .... *country* – Land
8. You put your books and papers into it. ....
9. You write with it on the board. ....
10. You draw lines with it. ....

Dialogue

Verbinde die deutschen Sätze mit allen passenden englischen Sätzen!

3.2 What to say in the classroom

Draw lines from the German to the English.

Ich habe mich verspätet.

Wie spricht man dieses Wort aus?

Bitte ganz langsam sprechen.

Wie heißt das auf Englisch?

Ich finde das prima.

Ich verstehe leider nicht.

Ich habe mein ... vergessen.

Kannst du das bitte noch einmal sagen?

Was heißt das auf Deutsch?

Could you speak slowly, please?

I'm sorry, I don't understand.

Great!

May I read?

Boring!

That's a good idea!

That's not true.

It's my turn

What does … mean?

Could you say that again, please?

I haven't done my homework.

What homework have we got?

I'm sorry I'm late.

What's that in German?

I have forgotten my …

What's that in English?

How do you pronounce this word?

Can I use your …, please?

Fine!

I don't think so!

May I write on the board?

Darf ich lesen?

Was heißt/bedeutet ...?

Welche Hausaufgaben haben wir auf?

Es ist langweilig.

Darf ich an die Wandtafel schreiben?

Das ist nicht wahr.

Ich bin an der Reihe.

Kann ich bitte dein ... benutzen?

3·3 The story of Sandy Small

Reading

Read aloud.

One day, Sandy meets a lion and he takes her to school on his back.

The teacher stops taking the register when she sees the little girl and the lion.

She looks at the lion, and all the other pupils look at the lion, wondering what the teacher is going to say.
The teacher says to the little girl, "You know you are not allowed to bring pets to school."
The lion begins to swish his tail – swish! swash! The little girl says, "This is not a pet. This is my friend who is coming to school with me."

The teacher still looks at the lion, but she says to the little girl, "What's his name then?"
"Noil," says the little girl. "His name is 'Noil', just 'Noil'."
She doesn't know what her friend's name is, so she turns his name backwards: lion – Noil.
The teacher writes the name down in the register. Noil.
Then she finishes calling the names.
"Sandy Small," she says.
"Yes," says the little girl.
"Noil," says the teacher.
"Yes," says the lion.

taking the register – die Namensliste kontrollieren

wonder – neugierig, gespannt sein

to be allowed – dürfen

pet – Haustier

tail

Fill in the gaps.

One day, Sandy .... a lion and he takes her to .... on his back. The .... stops taking the .... when she sees the little girl and the .... She looks at the .... and all the other .... look at the ...., wondering what the .... is going to say. The .... says to the little girl, "You know you are not allowed to bring pets to ...." The .... begins to swish his .... The little girl says, "This is my friend, who is coming to school with me." The .... asks his name. The little girl tells her, his name is Noil. The teacher writes the .... down in her book and the lion can stay in the classroom with Sandy.

3.4 Over to you: My class

Fill in.

In my class there are .... girls and .... boys. That makes .... children.

There are .... German boys and .... German girls. That makes .... German children.

There are .... boys and .... girls from other countries. That makes .... children from other countries.
In my class are girls and boys from

Diese und weitere Ländernamen findest du übrigens in Kapitel 9.

Ⓓ Germany	GB Great Britain	Ⓑ Belgium	Ⓔ Spain	GR Greece
TR Turkey	Ⓝ Norway	DK Denmark	Ⓟ Portugal	PL Poland
Ⓢ Sweden	Ⓕ France	NL The Netherlands	Ⓘ Italy	Ⓛ Luxembourg

In my classroom are .... table(s), ... chair(s), ... poster(s), ... picture(s), ... board(s), ... window(s), ... door(s), ... computer(s), ... overhead projector(s).

The objects in my schoolbag are:

1. .... 2. ....
3. .... 4. ....
5. .... 6. ....
7. ....

My best friend is ....

He / She is .... years old.
His / Her address is:

street ....

postal code .... city / town ....

My other friends are ....

4. Cardinal Numbers/Grundzahlen

Grammar

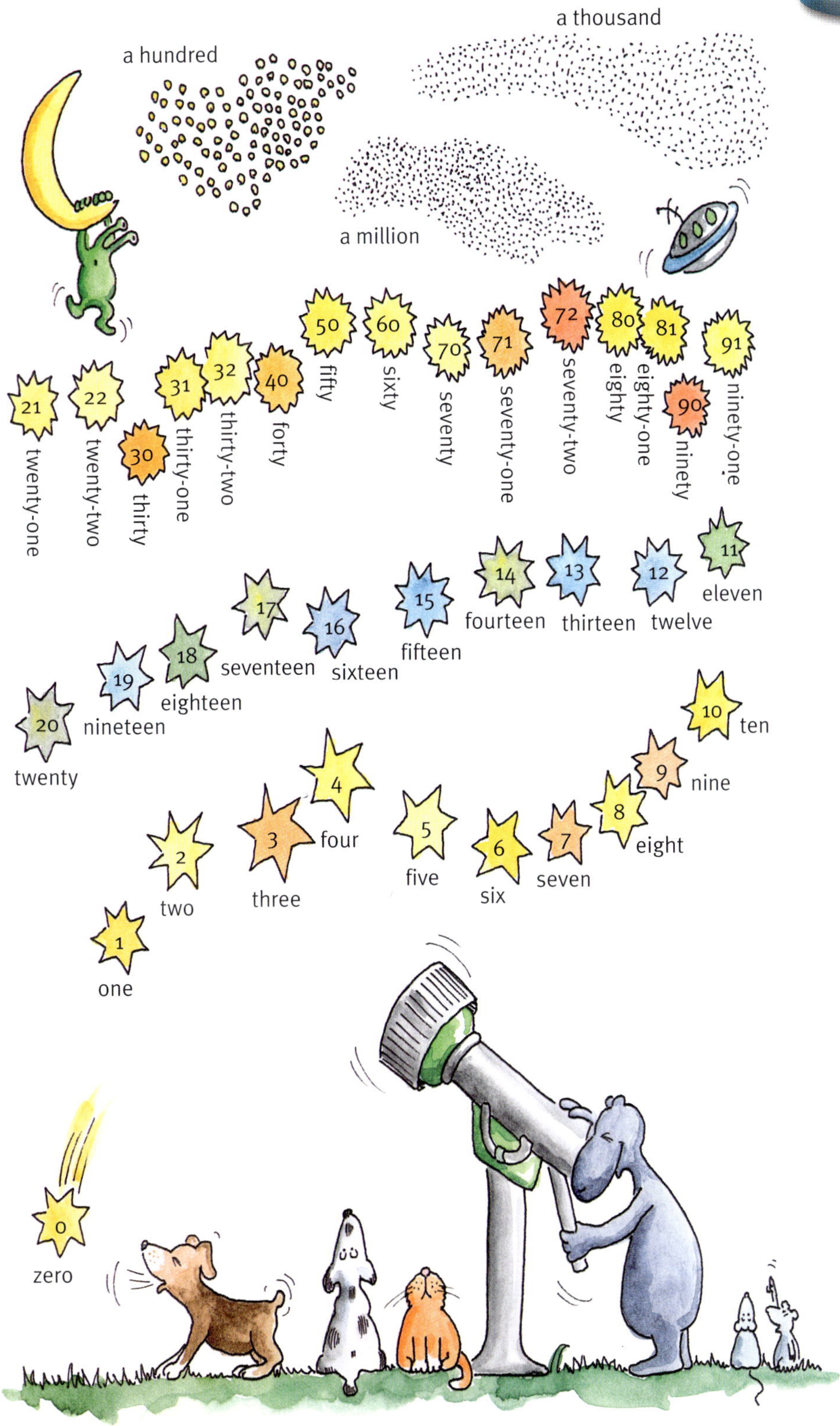

4.1 Let's play school

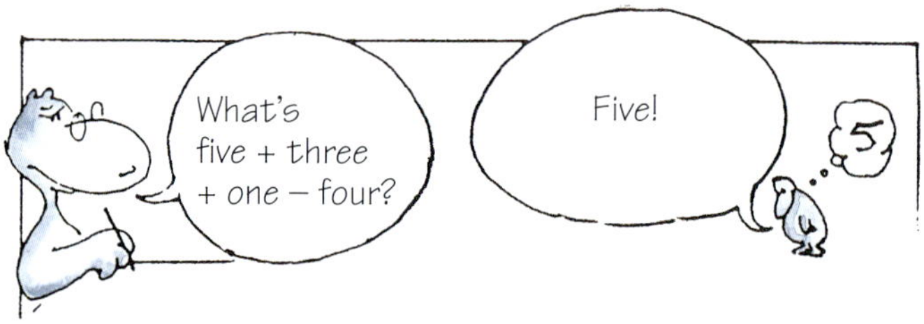

+ *plus* [plʌs]
– *minus* [maɪnəs]

1. nine – five – two + three = ...
2. eight + three – five = ...
3. twelve – five – one + four + two = ...
4. seven + five – two + one = ...
5. ten – .... = four
6. eleven + one – six – two – .... = two
7. .... + three – five + four = eleven
8. seven + two – .... + three = seven
9. ten – two – one + ... = ten

4.2 How many are there?

Trage die Antworten in Zahlen in die Kästen ein.

Find the correct answers to the number questions.

leg – Bein
quarter – Viertel
hour – Stunde

toe – Zehe
foot – Fuß

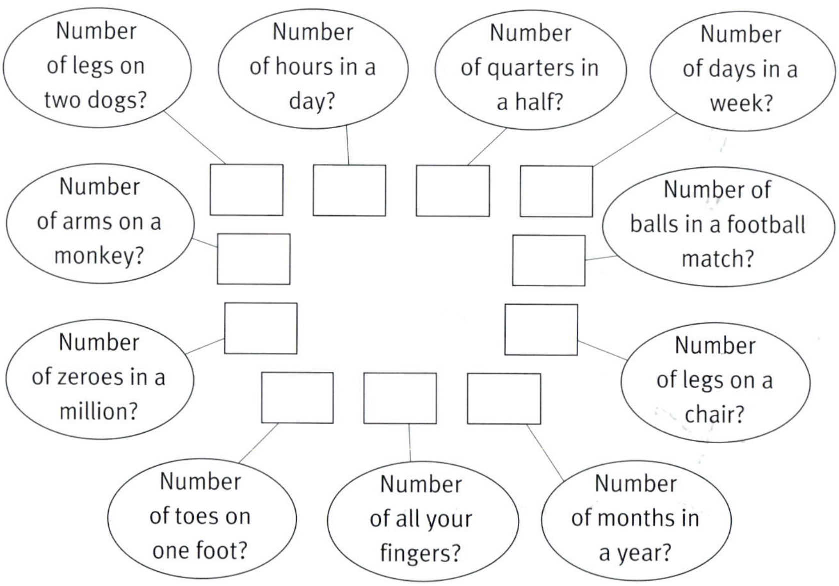

Zahlen beim Telefonieren

Null beim Telefonieren: ***o*** [əʊ]
My telephone number is 31044 (three-one-o-double four)
Doppelzahlen werden beim Telefonieren immer mit ***double*** angegeben: *4711 = four-seven-double one*

Info

4·3 Phone Numbers

Read the telephone numbers aloud.

103231	117720	148720	189480	215088
253865	345578	346445	423518	441005
472552	501447	650381	690931	720305

4·4 Telephoning

Say the telephone number and write it down.

A phone book

Nick: Double-three- o-seven

Brenda: fifty-eight thirty-two nineteen

Nancy: Double- seven-double- eight-double one

Fiona: ....

Janet: three-for- six-eight-ten

Colin: ....

Who is talking to whom? Follow the lines.

Wer telefoniert mit wem? Folge den Linien.

Nick is talking to Janet. Fiona is talking to Colin.
Brenda is talking to Nacy.

4.5 Over to you: Phoning a friend

Answer the questions.

1. Do you often phone your friends?
2. What do you talk about?
   homework – teachers – classmates – other friends – boys – girls

4.6 Numbers from 13 to 101

Read these numbers aloud.

13 thirteen	**14** fourteen	**15** fifteen	**16** sixteen	**17** seventeen	**18** eighteen	**19** nineteen
20 twenty	**21** twenty-one	**22** twenty-two	**30** thirty	**40** forty	**50** fifty	**60** sixty
70 seventy	**80** eighty	**90** ninety	**100** a hundred		**101** a hundred and one	

4.7 Pairs

Verbinde die ausgeschriebenen Zahlen mit den passenden Ziffern.

Match the pairs.

4.8 Over to you: Numbered details

In each of these details give the numbers in words. *Schreibe die Zahlen aus.*

My full name is ~~HESS~~ Anna-Luisa

In my full name there are Hess letters.

I am in class ~~5a~~ 5AP

I am 11 years and two months old.

In my class there are thirty girls and zero

boys, making .... altogether. *altogether – zusammen*

The school telephone number is ....

I am 165 cm tall. *tall – groß*

I get 25€ pocket money each ~~week.~~ ~~mot~~ months *pocket money – Taschengeld*

We have got a car. Its number is ~~FR~~ FR AL 721

What to say in a game?

Dialogue

Das willst du ausdrücken:	So sagst du es:
jemandem sagen, dass er anfangen soll	O.K. You start.
fragen, wer dran ist	Whose turn is it?
sagen, dass du selbst dran bist	It's my turn.
jemandem sagen, dass er dran ist	It's your turn.
jemanden fragen, wie viel er gewürfelt hat	How many have you got?
sagen, wie viel du gewürfelt hast	I've got 9 (8, ...)
Freude ausdrücken	Oh, great!
Ärger ausdrücken	Oh, no!
sagen, dass du gewonnen hast	Oh, I've won!
sagen, dass jemand Pech hat	Bad luck!
jemandem vorwerfen, dass er mogelt	Hey, you're cheating!
widersprechen	No, I'm not!
jemanden fragen, wie viele Punkte er hat	What's your score?

4·9 The word and number game

Beginne mit dem Würfeln bei Feld 1 und folge den Anweisungen. Du brauchst einen Würfel und Spielsteine.

Start at square one and follow the instructions. Play this by yourself or with a friend. You need dice and counters.

wear – tragen (Kleidung)
go forward ⟶
go back ⟵
No. – *number*

ride a bike – Fahrrad fahren

close – nahe

1 Everybody STARTs here	2 If your first name has an A in it, go to No. twelve. If not, go to No. three.	3 Say the numbers from one to ten.	4 If your birthday is in April, May or June, go to No. five. If not, go to No. seven.	5 How old are you? 
6 Go forward three.	7 If your name has an E in it, go to No. ten. If not, go to No. eleven.	8 If you are wearing something red, go to No. sixteen. If not, go to No. fourteen.	9 Count back from fifteen to ten.	10 Go back four.
11 If you like milk, go to No. eighteen. If not, go to No. nineteen. 	12 If it is raining today, go to No. fifteen. If not, go to No. seventeen.	13 What is seven plus thirty-eight?	14 If your birthday is in July, August or September, go to No. twenty-four. If not, go to No. twenty-three.	15 If there is a clock in your room, go to No. twenty-one. If not, go to No. twenty-two.
16 Count back from thirty to twenty. 	17 Go forward seven.	18 How many boys and girls are there in your class?	19 If you have any sisters, go back to No. five. If not, go to No. seven.	20 If you have a pet, go to No. twenty-four. If not, go to No. twenty-seven. 
21 If you can ride a bike, go to No. twenty-eight. If not, go to No. twenty-six.	22 What's your telephone number? 	23 Go forward eight.	24 What is ninety-nine minus fifty-two?	25 If you have any brothers, go to twenty-seven. If not, go to No. twenty-six. 
26 Count fifty to sixty. 	27 If you have long hair, go to No. thirty-two. If not, go to No. thirty.	28 How many chairs are there in your classroom?	29 You may go to Finish.	30 If your birthday is in October, November or December, go to No. twenty-two. If not, go to No. twenty-one.
31 If you live close to your school, go to No. thirty-three. If not, go to No. thirty-four.	32 What is twenty-two plus seventeen?	33 Go back twelve.	34 Boys go to No. twenty-four. Girls go to No. twenty-six.	**FINISH**

5. Ordinal Numbers/Ordnungszahlen

Ordnungszahlen bezeichnen die **Reihenfolge**: der Erste, die Zweite, der Dritte etc. Bei den Abkürzungen werden die letzten beiden Buchstaben hinter die Zahl geschrieben. Achte auf die Schreibung!

the first = 1st	the second = 2nd	the fourth = 4th
der Erste	der Zweite	der Vierte

Grammar

Waiting at the bus stop

1st	2nd	3rd	4th	5th	6th	7th	8th
the **first**	the **second**	the **third**	the fourth	the **fifth**	the sixth	the seventh	the eighth

!

9th	10th	11th	12th	13th	14th	15th	16th
the **ninth**	the tenth	the eleventh	the **twelfth**	the thir-teenth	the four-teenth	the fif-teenth	the six-teenth

17th	18th	19th	20th	21st	22nd	23rd
the seven-teenth	the eigh-teenth	the nine-teenth	the **twen-tieth**	the twenty-first	the twenty-second	the twenty-third

5.1 A car race

Match the ordinal numbers to the cars.

5.2 What am I?

Versuche herauszufinden, um welches Wort es sich handelt. Beachte das Wort answer.

Put the letters together and find the word.

My first letter is in queen but not in king.
It's q.

My second letter is in under but not in over.
It's ....

My third letter is in head but not in hair. It's ....

My fourth letter is in say and also in speak. It's ....

My fifth letter is in tree but not in flower. It's ....

My sixth letter is in ink and also in pencil. It's ....

My seventh letter is in horse and also in dog. It's ....

My eighth letter is in when but never in how. It's ....

And I always need an answer!

....

5.3 Twenty empty sacks

Reading

Read this and draw 20 pictures.

Put a pencil into the fourth sack.
Put a car into the seventh sack.
Put a ball into the tenth sack.
Put a shoe into the thirteenth sack.
Put a door into the sixteenth sack.
Put a bird into the twentieth sack.
Put a boat into the second sack.
Put a bucket into the eighth sack.
Put an apple into the third sack.
Put a handbag into the eighteenth sack.
Put a table into the nineteenth sack.
Put a bike into the seventeenth sack.
Put a stamp into the fifteenth sack.
Put a bottle into the twelfth sack.
Put a traffic light into the eleventh sack.
Put a carpet into the sixth sack.
Put a lamp into the ninth sack.
Put a girl into the first sack.
Put a house into the fifth sack.
Put a boy into the fourteenth sack.

bucket – Eimer

stamp – Briefmarke

traffic light – Ampel

carpet Teppich

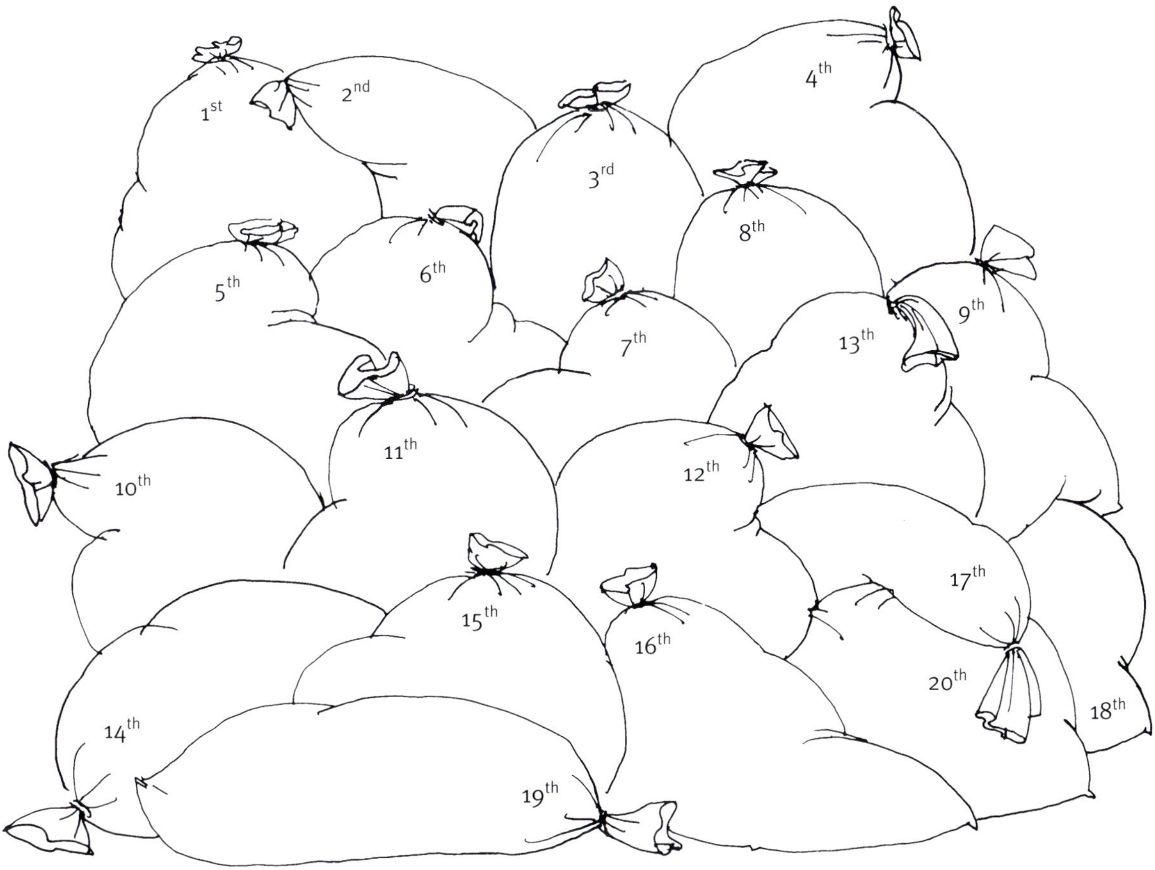

Grammar

Ordinal numbers

24th	the twenty-fourth
25th	the twenty-fifth
26th	the twenty-sixth
27th	the twenty-seventh
28th	the twenty-eighth
29th	the twenty-ninth
30th	the thirtieth
31st	the thirty-first
40th	the fourtieth
50th	the fiftieth
60th	the sixtieth
70th	the seventieth
80th	the eightieth
90th	the ninetieth
100th	the one hundredth
101st	the hundred and first

5.4 Matching exercise

Write the numbers into the boxes.

3rd 50th 1st 88th 12th

11th 18th 9th 36th 4th 57th 20th

the eighty-eighth	88th	the fourth		the fifty-seventh	
the twentieth		the thirty-sixth		the eighteenth	
the ninth		the third		the first	
the fiftieth		the twelfth		the eleventh	

5.5 Over to you: Personal details

Complete the sentences.

Today is the .... day of the month.

This month is the .... month of the year.

We are now in the .... hour of the day.

I have had my .... birthday and I am now in my .... year.

I am in my .... year at school.

I am the .... child in my family.

usually – gewöhnlich

I am usually the .... in my family to leave home in the morning.

I am usually the .... in my family to go to bed at night.

6. Days of the Week

The days of the week
Are seven in a row.
The days of the week
How quickly they go!

If snowy or rainy
Or sunny or grey,
The days of the week
Dance quickly away!

row – Reihe

quickly – schnell

Words

Wochentage sind Eigennamen und werden großgeschrieben.

6.1 Six days of the week

Mark the days. Which one is missing?

E	O	N	W	T	H	U
F	R	I	E	N	U	S
F	R	I	D	A	Y	A
S	M	O	N	D	A	Y
A	S	M	E	I	D	O
T	U	E	S	D	A	Y
U	N	A	D	O	I	M
R	D	S	A	A	U	O
D	A	U	Y	M	Y	N
A	Y	N	A	O	T	D
Y	I	D	D	N	U	A

It's ~~Tuesday~~ Thursday

6.2 The days of the week

Write the days of the week.

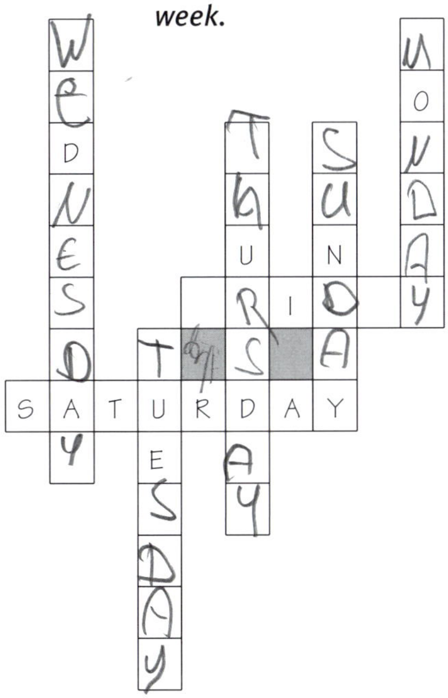

6.3 The week has seven days

Trage die Wochentage ein. Die Ordnungszahlen findest du übrigens auf den Seiten 23–26.

Find out the right days of the week.

April 2nd is a Thursday. April 1st is a ....

April 3rd is a Friday. April 4th is a ....

April 5th is a Sunday. March 31st is a ....

March 30th is a ....

6.4 A poem about the days of the week

Read aloud.

On Monday
I like going to school

On Tuesday
I like swimming

On Wednesday
I like doing maths

On Thursday
I like singing

On Friday
I like doing art

On Saturday
I like reading

On Sunday I like staying in bed
And drinking tea and eating

6.5 What does Fred do every week?

MON  On Mondays I do the shopping.

TUES .... 

WED   ....

THURS .... 

FRI  ....

SAT ....  

SUN   ....

do the shopping – work in the garden – watch TV – visit my friend – help my father – help my mother – go to the cinema – go to the sports club – listen to music – read a book – do my homework – sleep late – eat out at a restaurant – go to art school – go to the disco

to visit – besuchen
cinema – Kino
to sleep late – lange schlafen

6.6 Sunday is the best day of the week

Read what the girls and boys say about Sunday.

Jimmy: In the morning I sleep late.
Brenda: We play with Mum and Dad. They are at home on Sundays.
Tom: I go to church.
Sarah: We have a big breakfast but no dinner.
Jimmy: I go to the park with my friends.
Tom: We visit my grandmother on Sundays.
Brenda: On Sundays we eat out at a restaurant.
Michael: On Sundays we have a picnic in the garden.

church – Kirche

Write down in your exercise book what they do on Sundays.

Jimmy sleeps late and he …

Words 7. Months of the Year

7.1 Do you know the names of the months?

Fill in.

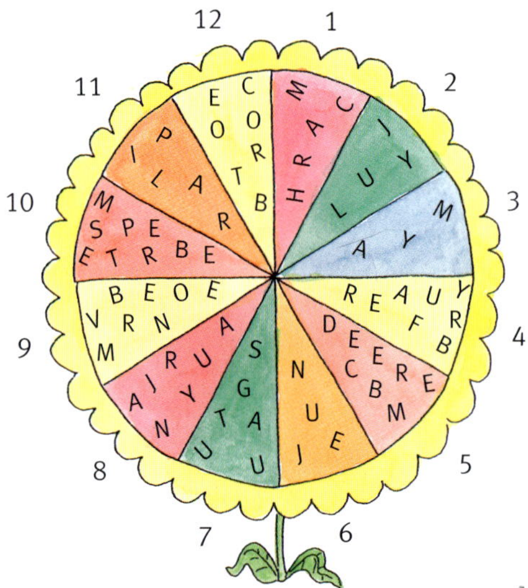

1. March
2. July
3. May
4. February
5. Decembre
6. June
7. August
8. January
9. Novembre
10. Septembre
11. Arpril
12. Octobre

7·2 The months

Fill in the names of the months.

January ....

....

....

7·3 Which month is it?

Fill in!

January is the first month of the year.

.... is the second month of the year.

.... is the fourth month of the year.

August is the .... month of the year.

September is the .... month of the year.

.... is the twelfth month of the year.

.... is the fifth month of the year.

.... is the eleventh month of the year.

March is the .... month of the year.

Info

The date

You can **write** the date like this:

You can **say** the date like this:

Dialogue

Talking about the date

Welches Datum haben wir heute?	→	What's the date today?
Wir haben den ersten Mai.	→	It's May (the) first. or It's the first of May.

7·4 What date is it?

Match the numbers and months in the two boxes with colours. Then write the dates.

third twentieth eighth ninth second thirtieth first thirty-first fourteenth twenty-second fifth

February May September June January October April July November August December March

2. 10. [green]	the second of October	October 2nd
20. 2. [blue]	....	....
1. 1. [white]	....	....
30. 3. [yellow]	....	....
3. 11. [red]	....	....
31. 12. [pink]	....	....
14. 5. [brown]	....	....

Schreibe die Daten auf, die noch übrig sind.

Now write the dates that are left.

22. 9.	....	....
9. 7.	....	....
5. 4.	....	....
8. 8.	....	....
2. 6.	....	....

7.5 A calendar

Look at the calendar and complete the sentences.

	JANUARY	FEBRUARY	MARCH	APRIL	MAY	JUNE
S	31 3 10 17 24	7 14 21 28	7 14 21 28	4 11 18 25	30 2 9 16 23	6 13 20 27
M	4 11 18 25	1 8 15 22	1 8 15 22 29	5 12 19 26	31 3 10 17 24	7 14 21 28
T	5 12 19 26	2 9 16 23	2 9 16 23 30	6 13 20 27	4 11 18 25	1 8 15 22 29
W	6 13 20 27	3 10 17 24	3 10 17 24 31	7 14 21 28	5 12 19 26	2 9 16 23 30
Th	7 14 21 28	4 11 18 25	4 11 18 25	1 8 15 22 29	6 13 20 27	3 10 17 24
F	1 8 15 22 29	5 12 19 26	5 12 19 26	2 9 16 23 30	7 14 21 28	4 11 18 25
S	2 9 16 23 30	6 13 20 27	6 13 20 27	3 10 17 24	1 8 15 22 29	5 12 19 26

	JULY	AUGUST	SEPTEMBER	OCTOBER	NOVEMBER	DECEMBER
S	4 11 18 25	1 8 15 22 29	5 12 19 26	31 3 10 17 24	7 14 21 28	5 12 19 26
M	5 12 19 26	2 9 16 23 30	6 13 20 27	4 11 18 25	1 8 15 22 29	6 13 20 27
Tu	6 13 20 27	3 10 17 24 31	7 14 21 28	5 12 19 26	2 9 16 23 30	7 14 21 28
W	7 14 21 28	4 11 18 25	1 8 15 22 29	6 13 20 27	3 10 17 24	1 8 15 22 29
Th	1 8 15 22 29	5 12 19 26	2 9 16 23 30	7 14 21 28	4 11 18 25	2 9 16 23 30
F	2 9 16 23 30	6 13 20 27	3 10 17 24	1 8 15 22 29	5 12 19 26	3 10 17 24 31
S	3 10 17 24 31	7 14 21 28	4 11 18 25	2 9 16 23 30	6 13 20 27	4 11 18 25

● Fred ◆ Mum ■ Aunt Mary ◊ Pam ○ Dad

Mum's birthday is on the twenty-second of September.

Dad's birthday is on ....

Fred's birthday is on ....

Aunt Mary's birthday is on ....

Pam's birthday is on ....

> Bei der Frage, wann man geboren wurde, gebraucht man im Englischen immer ***was***/***were*** (Past Tense).

7.6 Over to you: Talking about your family

Answer the questions.

When is your birthday? On the .... of ....

When is your mother's birthday? On the .... of ....

When is your father's birthday? On the .... of ....

When were you born? In .... (year).

When was your father born? In ....

When was your mother born? In ....

7.7 Birthday rhyme time

Fill in.

dish – Platte / Teller

The candles are lit.
The cake's on its dish.
It's time to make my
birthday ....!

Today's the date!
I'm feeling great!
What day's today?
It's my ....!

It's fun to mix
It's fun to make,
It's fun to bake
A birthday ....!

7.8 Pen friends

Michael and Claudia are pen friends. Michael lives in Edinburgh, Scotland. Claudia lives in Kiel, Germany. Fill in the blanks.

Dear ...., 

Many thanks for your ....  . I hope you and your family are well. We are all fine. I'm writing this letter on .... 

of January.

It's ....  here now. It's ....  a lot at the moment. I can't ....  this .... 

, so I'm staying at home listening to  ...., watching ....  and writing this letter.

Next .... 

is my ....  and Mum is making me a big ....  .

She's got eleven ....  for it. All my friends will come to my .... 

and we'll ....  and ....  . My birthday also means more ....  .

Please write soon!

Best wishes

Michael

Reading

7·9 Susan's birthday

Read the text and answer the questions.

October the 11th is a great day for Susan. It's her birthday. She's eleven. In the morning she opens her birthday cards. She has seventeen cards from her family and her friends. From her mum and dad she gets a new bike, and from her brother Bob a wonderful book about horses. Susan likes horses very much. Aunt Mary gives her £ 25. "You can buy some jeans or T-shirts with it," she says. Susan is very happy. At half past three there's a big birthday party at her house. All her friends are there. They eat birthday cake and play a lot of games. They also dance to Susan's favourite music. Susan dances with Peter. At nine o'clock she is very tired – and very happy. "What a great day," she thinks.

1. When is Susan's birthday? ....
2. How old is she? ....
3. What does she do in the morning? ....
4. How many cards does she get? ....
5. What does she get from her family? ....
6. What do the boys and girls do at Susan's party? ....

7·10 Over to you: What do you do on your birthday?

Write sentences in your exercise book about your birthday.

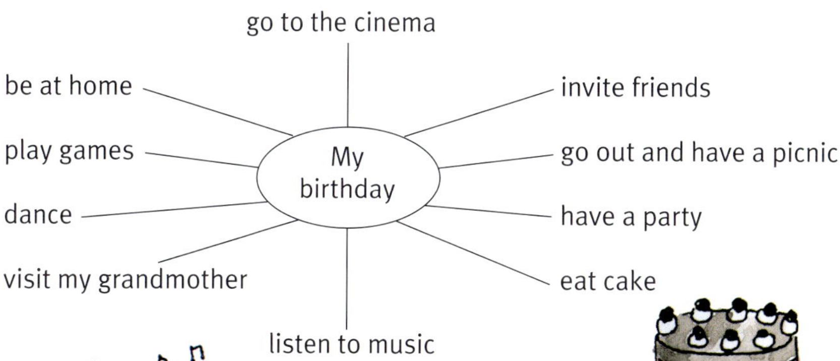

8. The Time

Words

Clocks and watches

1 wristwatch
2 alarm clock
3 station clock
4 church clock
5 grandfather clock
6 pocket watch

Große Uhren heißen clock, kleine heißen watch.
Das Ziffernblatt heißt face und die Zeiger hands.

8.1 What is it?

Fill in.

....

....

....

....

Wie man die Zeit angibt

Info

to – vor
past – nach

Ab der 31. Minute heißt es **to**.

(a) quarter to = Viertel vor

It's one o'clock.
full hours = o'clock

Bis einschließlich der 30. Minute heißt es **past**.

(a) quarter past = Viertel nach

Examples:

It's five o'clock.

It's five past five.

It's ten past five.

It's quarter past five.

It's twenty past five.

It's twenty-five past five.

It's half past five.

It's twenty-five to six.

It's twenty to six.

It's quarter to six.

It's ten to six.

It's five to six.

8.2 What's the time?

1.

2.

3.

4.

5.

6.

7.

8.

1. twenty past eight ....
2. ....
3. ....
4. ....
5. ....
6. ....
7. ....
8. ....
9. ....

9.

10.

11.

12.

13.

14.

15.

16.

9. ....
10. ....
11. ....
12. ....
13. ....
14. ....
15. ....
16. ....

8.3 Drawing the time

Draw the hands of the clocks.

Zeichne die Zeiger der Uhr jeweils nach der angegebenen Uhrzeit ein.

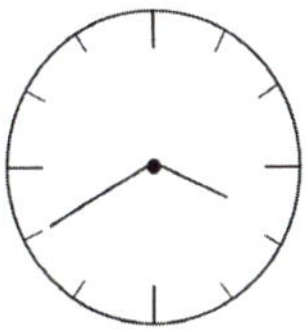
It's twenty to four

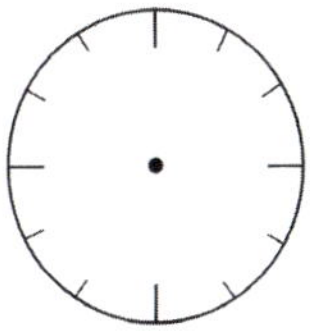
It's ten to two

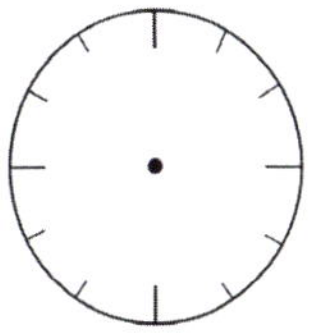
It's five to seven

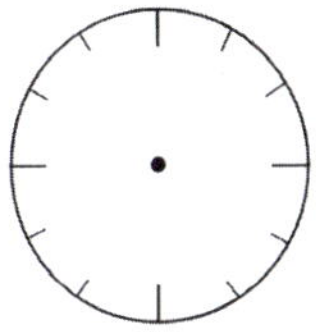
It's twenty-five to ten

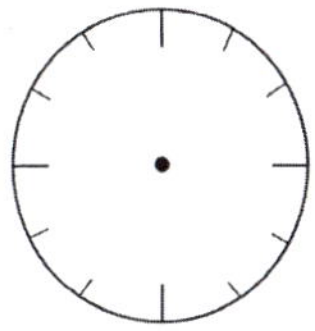
It's twenty to eight

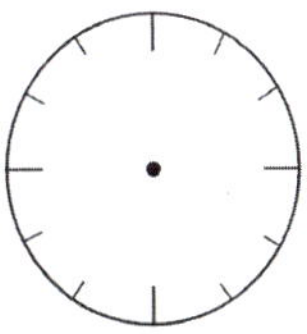
It's five past seven

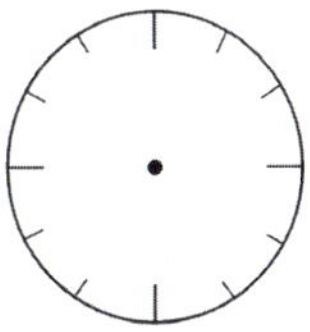
It's twenty-five past one

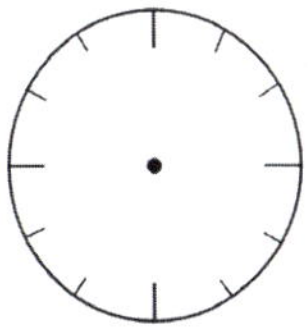
It's ten past eleven

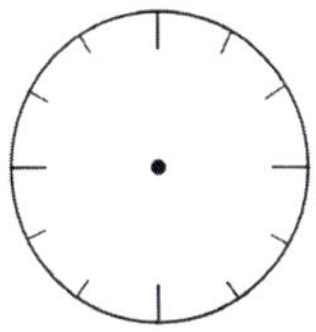
It's twenty past three

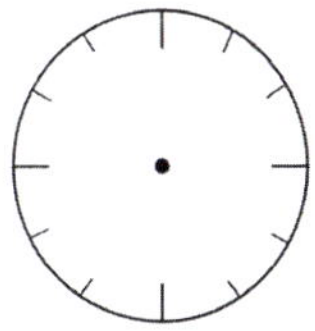
It's twenty-five past nine

How to ask and tell the time

Dialogue

fragen, wie spät es ist

What time is it, please?
Can you tell me the time, please?

sagen, wie spät es ist
volle Stunden
halbe Stunden
Viertelstunden
auf 5 Minuten genau
Minutenangaben

It's
... o'clock.
half past ...
(a) quarter past / to ...
five / ten past ...
twenty past ...
twenty-five past / to ...
twenty / ten / five to ...
one **minute** past ...
three **minutes** to ...
sixteen **minutes** to ...

sagen, dass
es genau ... ist
es ungefähr ... ist
man leider keine Uhr hat
man die Uhrzeit nicht weiß

It's
exactly ...
about ...
I'm sorry, I haven't got a watch.
I don't know.

! Bei 1 – 4, 6 – 9, 11 – 14, 16 – 19, 21 – 24 ist das Wort ***minute/minutes*** als Ergänzung notwendig.

8.4 Saturday morning at the Carters'

Setze die Verben ein und schreibe die Uhrzeit aus.

Put in the correct form of the verbs and write the time in words.

Mrs. Carter (to get up) gets up at (a) quarter past seven.

Mr. Carter gets up at ....

At  .... Mr. and Mrs. Carter (to have) .... breakfast.

After breakfast Mr. Carter (to read) .... the newspaper.
Mrs. Carter (to call) .... the children.

sleepyhead – Schlafmütze

Susan (to get up) .... at once, but Tom is a sleepyhead.

He (to lie) .... in bed until ....

At  .... Mrs. Carter (to go) .... into the kitchen and (to make)....................... breakfast for the children.

At  .... Susan and Tom (to take) the breakfast things to the kitchen.

Mr. Carter (to do) .... the washing-up, and Susan (to help) .... her father.

At  .... they (to go) .... shopping.

Susan and Tom (to play) .... with their friends.

At  .... they all (to sit down) .... to lunch in the dining room.

9. Countries, Peoples and Languages

A map of Europe

Info

In the United Kingdom live English people,
Welsh people (Waliser),
Scottish people (Schotten)
and Northern Irish people (Nordiren).

Here are some more countries

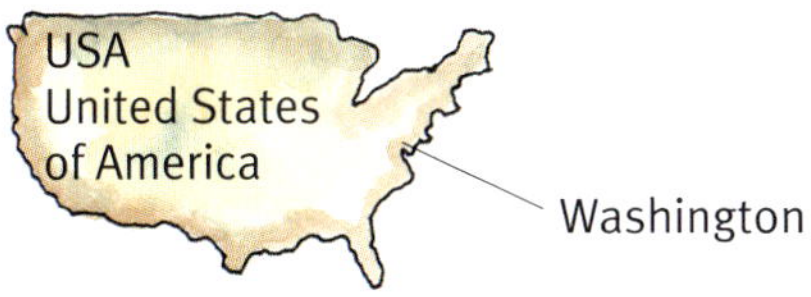

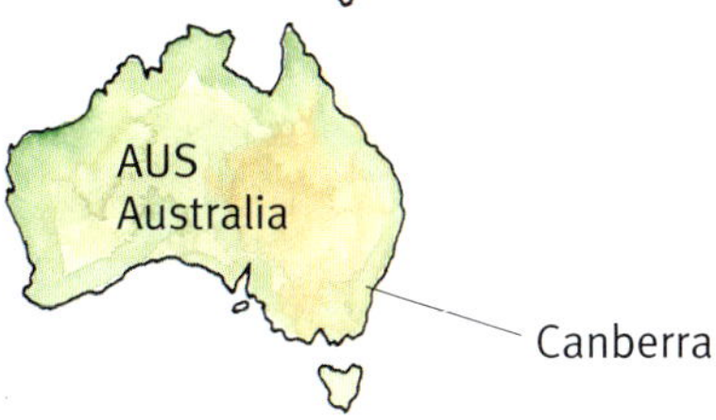

people – Volk
peoples – Völker
map – Landkarte

9.1 Holidays

Wo verbringen sie ihre Ferien?

Where are they spending their holidays? Write in your exercise book.

Alec Cindy Bill Patty Rick Susan Ramesh Sally

Example:
Alec is in Spain.

9.2 Cars from other countries

Colour the pictures.

Colour the car from Britain red. The car from Germany is green. Colour the car from Austria brown. The car from Italy is blue. The car from Switzerland is black. Colour the car from Sweden yellow. The car from America is pink. The car from France is orange.

People from other countries

Words

1. Germany	2. Denmark	3. Finland	4. France	country
German	Danish	Finnish	French	nationality
German	Danish	Finnish	French	language

5. Spain	6. Greece	7. England	8. America (USA)	country
Spanish	Greek	English	American	nationality
Spanish	Greek	English	American English	language

9. Sweden	10. Portugal	11. Austria	12. Norway	country
Swedish	Portuguese	Austrian	Norwegian	nationality
Swedish	Portuguese	German	Norwegian	language

13. Holland	14. Turkey	15. Italy	16. Switzerland	country
Dutch	Turkish	Italian	Swiss	nationality
Dutch	Turkish	Italian	German, French, Italian	language

9.3 What can you say about these people?

1. Horst is from Germany. He is German and speaks German.

Go on like this with the others. Write in your exercise book.

9.4 European friends

1 2 3 4 5 6 7 8

Peggy	Maria	Pit	Pierre	Helgo	Mario	Sam	Xaver
Great Britain	Spain	Holland	France	Switzer-land	Italy	USA	Austria
Liver-pool	Madrid	Amster-dam	Paris	Zürich	Rome	New York	Vienna
English French	Spanish German	Dutch English German	French English	German French Italian	Italian	English a little German	German Polish
2 brothers 1 sister	4 brothers 2 sisters	1 sister	2 brothers	1 brother 1 sister	2 sisters	1 brother	3 sisters
7 years old	12 years old	10 years old	14 years old	15 years old	11 years old	9 years old	13 years old

Ask questions about the girls and boys. Write in your exercise book.

1. Peggy

Dialogue

Example:

What's your name? ⟷ My name is Peggy.
Where are you from? ⟷ I'm from Great Britain.
Where in Great Britain? ⟷ From Liverpool.
What language do you speak? ⟷ English and French.
How many brothers and sisters have you got? ⟷ I've got two brothers and one sister.
How old are you? ⟷ I'm seven.

9.5 Facts about people

Schreib auf, was du über die Mädchen und Jungen weißt.

Write down what you know about the girls and boys.

Number 1: Her name **is** Peggy. She **lives** in Liverpool. She **has got** two brothers and one sister. She **comes from** Great Britain. She **speaks** English and French. She **is** seven years old.

9.6 A world tour

Du kannst alleine oder mit Freunden spielen. Du brauchst einen Würfel und für jeden Mitspieler einen Stein. Sieger ist, wer zuerst am Ziel (25) ist.

You can play on your own or with friends. You need a dice, and a piece for each player. The players throw the dice in turn. You may move forward as many squares as the number on the dice. Follow the instructions in the squares. The winner is the first one to reach the finish (25).

engine trouble – Maschinenschaden; *valid* – gültig; *fall sick* – krank werden; *high temperature* – Fieber; *traffic* – Verkehr; *straight* – direkt

9.7 Over to you: My country Germany

A map of Germany

1. Some place names, rivers and seas are different in German and English. Can you fill in the English names?

Baltic Sea
Cologne
Hanover
North Sea
Danube
Munich
Nuremberg
Rhine

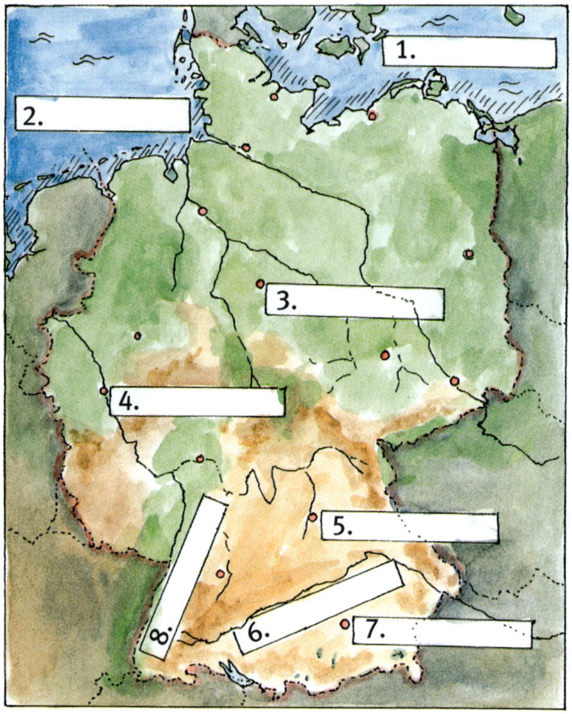

A compass

North
Northwest
Northeast
West
East
Southwest
Southeast
South

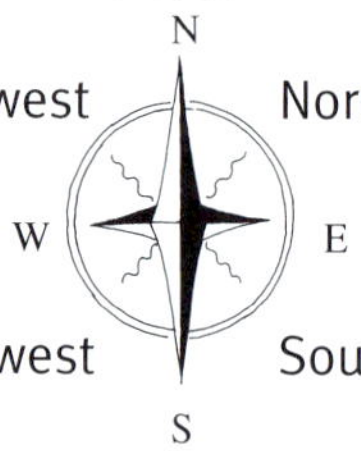

2. Show me Germany:

capital – Hauptstadt

Mark the capital and your town / village on the map.
Mark three famous places in your country.
Mark the longest river and the highest mountains.

3. About my country:

currency – Währung

How many people are there in Germany?
What language do the people speak?
What currency do they use?
Who do you think is the most famous person in the country?

4. Where do you live? Use the words from the list.

My town / city is	in the north of in the east of in the south of in the west of	It's	northeast of northwest of southeast of southwest of	It's	near (Kiel) between (Nuremberg and Munich) on the (Rhine)

10. Singular and Plural / Singular und Plural

Bildung und Aussprache des Plurals

Der Plural (Mehrzahl) wird normalerweise gebildet, indem man ein **-s** an die Form des Singulars (Einzahl) hängt.
Wenn der Singular mit den „harten" Konsonanten **-p, -t, -k** oder **-f** endet, hört sich das **-s** im Plural wie das Zischen einer Schlange an (stimmloses s):  [s]

Wenn der Singular mit den „weichen" Konsonanten **-b, -d, -g, -l, -m, -n, -v** oder mit einem Vokal endet, hört sich das **-s** im Plural wie das Summen einer Biene an (stimmhaftes s):  [z]

Grammar

Singular	 a boy	 a cat	 a pen	 a bird
Plural	 two boys	 four cats	 eight pens	 lots of birds

10.1 How many are there?

Write some sentences in your exercise book.

There are two boys, nine birds, …

Besondere Pluralformen

Bei einigen Wörtern endet der Singular mit einem **Zischlaut:-sh, -x, -ss, -ch.** Bei diesen wird der Plural mit **-es** gebildet.
Die Aussprache ist [iz], also mit i und weichem s.

Singular

one dish

one box

one class

a watch

Plural

three dishes

three boxes

two classes

four watches

Wenn der Singular mit einem **Konsonanten (Mitlaut) und -y** endet, zum Beispiel bei *baby*, dann wird das -y- im Plural zu einem -ie-. Die Pluralform endet dann mit **-ies.** Sie wird [i:z] gesprochen, also mit langem i und weichem s.

Singular

one baby

a fly

a pony

Plural

two babies

three flies

two ponies

Wenn der Singular jedoch mit einem **Vokal (Selbstlaut) und -y** endet, zum Beispiel bei *boy*, dann wird im Plural ganz normal nur das -s angehängt. Es wird weich gesprochen: [z]

Singular

a key

boy

donkey

Plural

five keys

three boys

two donkeys

Wenn der Singular auf ein **stummes e** endet, spricht man das -es im Plural wie bei Konsonanten und y mit i und weichem s: [iz]

Singular

one horse

a bridge

one orange

one rose

Plural

two horses

two bridges

four oranges

six roses

10.2 Find the singular forms

Write the singular form of the word you find in each row.

In jeder waagrechten Reihe steht ein englisches Wort im Plural. Schreibe die Singularformen auf.

1. match	S	B	D	O	M	A	T	C	H	E	S	
	O	M	O	N	K	E	Y	S	R	M	S	2. ………
3. ………	L	A	T	K	K	E	Y	S	I	T	R	
	L	O	M	D	I	C	A	R	S	S	K	4. ………
5. ………	F	L	I	D	R	E	S	S	E	S	F	
	G	I	R	I	D	I	S	H	E	S	K	6. ………
7. ………	A	N	B	A	B	I	E	S	B	I	S	
	T	S	I	E	C	P	O	N	I	E	S	8. ………
9. ………	P	A	G	E	S	A	H	N	E	U	A	
	B	O	Y	S	U	M	A	N	S	E	Q	10. ………
11. ………	O	R	O	S	E	S	I	E	S	E	N	
	A	T	P	F	O	R	F	L	I	E	S	12. ………
13. ………	S	P	A	S	P	O	O	N	S	E	I	
	C	A	B	R	I	D	G	E	S	U	M	14. ………
15. ………	B	I	R	T	H	H	O	R	S	E	S	
	S	U	D	O	N	K	E	Y	S	A	T	16. ………
17. ………	A	B	C	B	O	X	E	S	Z	Y	W	
	S	O	H	O	U	S	E	S	F	G	K	18. ………
19. ………	U	N	I	F	O	R	M	S	U	U	M	
	A	B	C	D	E	F	O	X	E	S	I	20. ………
21. ………	F	H	G	L	A	S	S	E	S	G	T	

10.3 Pronunciation exercise

Read aloud.

s

[s]			
ship	→	ship**s**
cat	→	cat**s**
clock	→	clock**s**
pet	→	pet**s**

[z]		
boy	→	boy**s**
egg	→	egg**s**
word	→	word**s**
tree	→	tree**s**
apple	→	apple**s**
train	→	train**s**

[iz]		
house	→	house**s**
orange	→	orange**s**
horse	→	horse**s**
blouse	→	blouse**s**
vase	→	vase**s**

es

[iz]		
bus	→	bus**es**
church	→	church**es**
box	→	box**es**
watch	→	watch**es**
kiss	→	kiss**es**
dress	→	dress**es**

[i:z]		
lady	→	lad**ies**
city	→	cit**ies**
baby	→	bab**ies**
body	→	bod**ies**
country	→	countr**ies**
story	→	stor**ies**

10.4 A house in the country

How many things can you see? Write in your exercise book.

I can see four boys. I can see …

Besondere Schreibweisen

Wenn das Wort im Singular auf **-f** oder auf **-fe** endet, wird im Plural daraus **-ves**.

Grammar

Singular

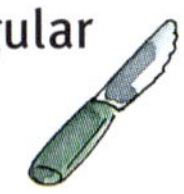
a knife

a loaf of bread

a leaf

a calf

a thief

Plural

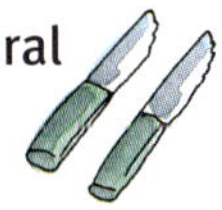
two kni**ves**

loa**ves**

lea**ves**

a lot of cal**ves**

two thie**ves**

Unregelmäßige Pluralbildung

Bei einigen ganz wenigen Nomen wird die Pluralform unregelmäßig gebildet.

man	→	men	ox	→	oxen
woman [ˈwʊmən]	→	women [ˈwɪmɪn]	mouse	→	mice
			sheep	→	sheep
child	→	children	fish	→	fish
tooth	→	teeth	goose	→	geese
foot	→	feet	penny	→	pence

10.5 Irregular forms in the plural

Write the plural forms under the pictures.

fish ....

....

....

....

....

....

....

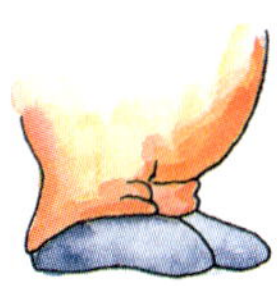
....

....

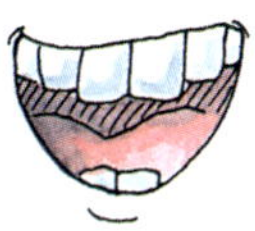
....

....

10.6 What can you see?

Fill in.

 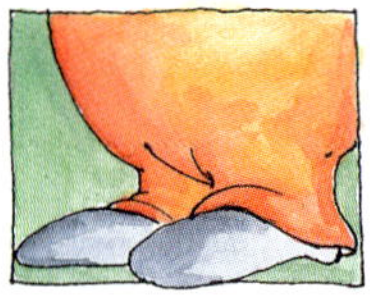  

men ………… ………… ………… …………

………… ………… ………… …………

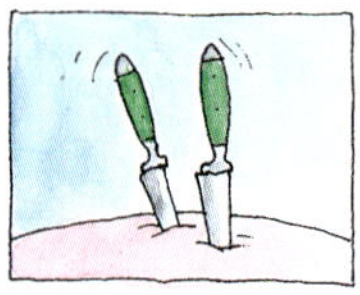   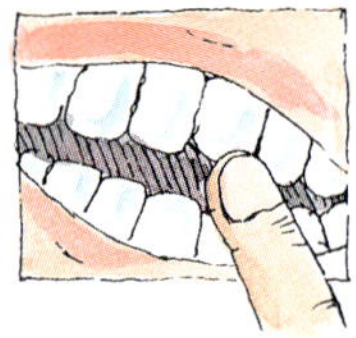

………… ………… ………… …………

10.7 Plural final test

Setze die Nomen und Verben in den Plural; die Formen von to be *findest du übrigens auf Seite 64.*

Change the noun word and the form of the verb from singular to plural.

Singular		Plural
1. The book is on the desk.	→	The books are on the desk.
2. The class ends at two o'clock.	→	The classes end at two o'clock.
3. The woman is in the shop.	→	…………
4. The child plays with the dog.	→	…………
5. The cat runs after the mouse.	→	…………
6. The bus is full.	→	…………
7. The man is busy.	→	…………
8. The woman is also busy.	→	…………
9. The mouse runs into a hole.	→	…………
10. The boy plays in the park.	→	…………
11. The thief steals money.	→	…………
12. The dish is on the table.	→	…………
13. The shelf is full of books.	→	…………
14. The policeman catches the thief.	→	…………

busy – beschäftigt

hole – Loch

to steal – stehlen

to catch – fangen

11. S-Genitive and Of-Genitive/Der Genitiv

S-Genitiv

Mit dem Genitiv (Besitzfall) drückst du einen Besitz oder eine Zugehörigkeit aus. Während es im Deutschen nur einen Genitiv gibt, gibt es im Englischen zwei.
Du verwendest den **s-Genitiv**, wenn der Besitzer eine **Person** oder ein **Tier** ist (nach dem Besitzer fragst du mit „wessen").
Im **Singular (= ein einziger Besitzer)** bildest du den s-Genitiv, indem du an das Nomen, das den Besitzer bezeichnet, einen Apostroph **'** und ein **-s** anhängst.

Grammar

The girl's book
(das Buch des Mädchens)

The girl's books
(die Bücher des Mädchens)

The man's house
(das Haus des Mannes)

The man's houses
(die Häuser des Mannes)

The dog's kennel
(die Hütte des Hundes)

11.1 Peter has a lot of work to do

What must he do?

He must fetch his father's newspaper.

his father
to fetch – holen

He must clean ....

the children

He must make ....

the family

He must wash ....

the neighbour
neighbour – Nachbar

He must brush ....

Debbie
to brush – bürsten

He must repair ....

Tom
to repair – reparieren

Aussprache

Das **-'s** des Genitivs wird gesprochen wie das Plural-**s**.

Jack's friend / my parents' house [ks] [ts]	[s]	=	stimmlos nach stimmlosen Konsonanten
father's car / the boys' bikes [z] [z]	[z]	=	stimmhaft nach stimmhaften Lauten
the mouse's teeth [iz]	[iz]	=	nach Zischlauten

Info

Grammar

Mehrere Besitzer: Beim **regelmäßig** gebildeten Plural, wenn also die Pluralform des Wortes auf **-s** endet, wird nur ein **Apostroph '** an das Wort angehängt.

The girls' book (das Buch der Mädchen)

The girls' books (die Bücher der Mädchen)

My parents' home (das Heim meiner Eltern)

My brothers' bedroom (das Schlafzimmer meiner Brüder)

Mehrere Besitzer: Beim **unregelmäßigen** Plural wird wie an die Einzahl ein **Apostroph ' + s** an das Hauptwort angehängt.

The men's houses (die Häuser der Männer)

The children's dolls (die Puppen der Kinder)

The women's bags (die Taschen der Frauen)

11.2 Whose is it?

1. house / Mr. Brown

2. satchel / Ben

3. books / girls

4. trousers / children

5. doll / Peter

6. table / Susan

7. watch / man

8. hats / woman

Form sentences and write in your exercise book.

Example: 1. It's Mr. Brown's house.

Of-Genitiv

Handelt es sich bei dem „Besitzer" um einen **Gegenstand**, so musst du den **of-Genitiv** verwenden. Damit zeigst du, zu welchem Gegenstand ein anderer Gegenstand gehört. Du bildest den of-Genitiv, indem du vor den „Besitzer" ***of*** stellst.

Grammar

The roof of the house
(das Dach des Hauses)

The window of the house
(das Fenster des Hauses)

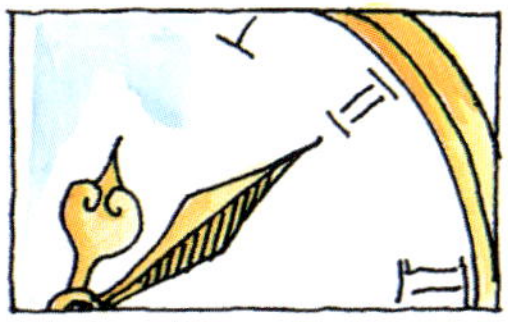

The hands of the clock
(die Zeiger der Uhr)

11.3 Cleaning day

cleaning day – Großreinemachen

Fred has a very hard day today. He must clean

floor / kitchen the floor of the kitchen.

seats / chairs ....

windows / house ....

top / sideboard ....

walls / sitting room ....

carpet / bedroom ....

11.4 Mixed exercise: s-Genitive or of-Genitive?

Form sentences with the words.

1. butcher / window / is broken The butcher's window is broken.
2. colour / house / is yellow ....
3. arm / Emily / doll / is broken ....
4. father / car / is in the garage ....
5. the children / room / is upstairs ....
6. mother / must clean / girls / dresses ....
7. door / car / is very dirty ....
8. the women / clothes / are very expensive ....

12. Personal Pronouns (subject case) / Personalpronomen

Grammar

Die Personalpronomen (persönlichen Fürwörter) stehen als **Ersatz für Personen, Sachen, Pflanzen und Tiere,** z. B. um Wiederholungen zu vermeiden. Du verwendest die **Subjektsform** des Personalpronomens, wenn du in einem Satz ein **Nomen ersetzen** möchtest, das **Subjekt** (Satzgegenstand) **des Satzes** ist.

Die Formen der Personalpronomen

Singular

1. Person

I

Du sprichst über dich selbst. *I* wird immer großgeschrieben! *I am happy.*

2. Person

you

Du redest eine andere Person an. *You are late.*

3. Person

he she it

Du sagst etwas über eine männliche Person. *He is my brother.*

Du sagst etwas über eine weibliche Person. *She is my sister.*

Du sagst etwas über ein Tier, eine Pflanze oder einen Gegenstand. *It is a box.*

Plural

1. Person

we

Du sagst etwas über dich selbst und andere Personen. *We are friends.*

2. Person

you

Du sagst etwas zu mehreren Personen. *You are my friends.*

3. Person

they

Du sagst etwas über:

- mehrere Personen
  They are my teachers.
- mehrere Sachen
  They are my books.
- mehrere Pflanzen
  They are beautiful flowers.
- mehrere Tiere
  They are horses.

Beispiele

1. *Maria sees the boy.*
   She sees the boy.

Das Subjekt ***Maria*** wird durch das Personalpronomen ***she*** ersetzt.

2. *The children buy presents.*
   They buy presents.

Das Subjekt ***the children*** wird durch das Personalpronomen ***they*** ersetzt.

Grammar

12.1 Replacing exercise

Replace the words in blue by the personal pronouns.

Ersetze die blau markierten Wörter durch die richtigen Personalpronomen.

1. Maria and I like speaking English. — We like speaking English.
2. The book is on the desk. — .... is on the desk.
3. Maria's sister is not at home. — ....
4. Kevin is a good pupil. — ....
5. John and his brother are in the cafeteria. — ....
6. Maria has got one sister and two brothers. — ....
7. The weather is very cold today. — ....
8. The horses run into the field. — ....

field – Acker, Feld

12.2 The new house

Put in the personal pronouns.

Is the house very big? — Yes, it is.

How many rooms has the house got? — .... has got 8 rooms.

Are the rooms big? — Yes, they are.

Is the hall very long? — No, ... isn't.

Can David put his car into the garage? — Yes, ... can.

Can Linda cook in the basement? — No, ... can't.

Can the children play in the sitting room? — No, ... can't.

Are the windows large? — No, ... aren't.

hall – Diele, Flur

basement – Kellergeschoss

12.3 Personal pronouns

Replace the subject in the following sentences by its personal pronoun.

1. Fred is swimming in the lake. He
2. Mr. Smith is in his office. ....
3. John and his brother are in the cafeteria. ....
4. This book is new. ....
5. Those books are new. ....
6. The girl opens the door for me. ....
7. Karen and I like to learn English. ....
8. The weather is very cold today. ....
9. His son and daughter live with him. ....
10. Ben is a good student. ....
11. Sarah and I want to speak English well. ....
12. Ben is a good swimmer. ....
13. Oliver and Joe are repairing the cassette. ....
14. The girl takes the toy. ....
15. Jack cleans his room. ....
16. My father's pipe is in the kitchen. ....
17. My father and I repair the bike. ....
18. The boys are doing their homework. ....
19. The telephone doesn't work. ....
20. My sister has a boyfriend. ....
21. Amy is here, too, Amy is John's friend. ....

12.4 More personal pronouns

Write the personal pronouns in the gaps.

1. Fred: .... am Fred from Germany.
2. Where are you from? .... are from Hamburg.
3. There is Sarah. .... is cleaning the bike.
4. Where is my book? .... isn't here.
5. The children have been playing in the park. .... are going home.
6. Look at that car! .... is very old.
7. Are .... Tom, the new boy?
8. Sharon and Wendy, come here, please. .... are too noisy.
9. Where are .... from? .... am from London.
10. Look at those pencils! .... are green.

A family tree

Words

Hello! My name is Kate and this is my family.

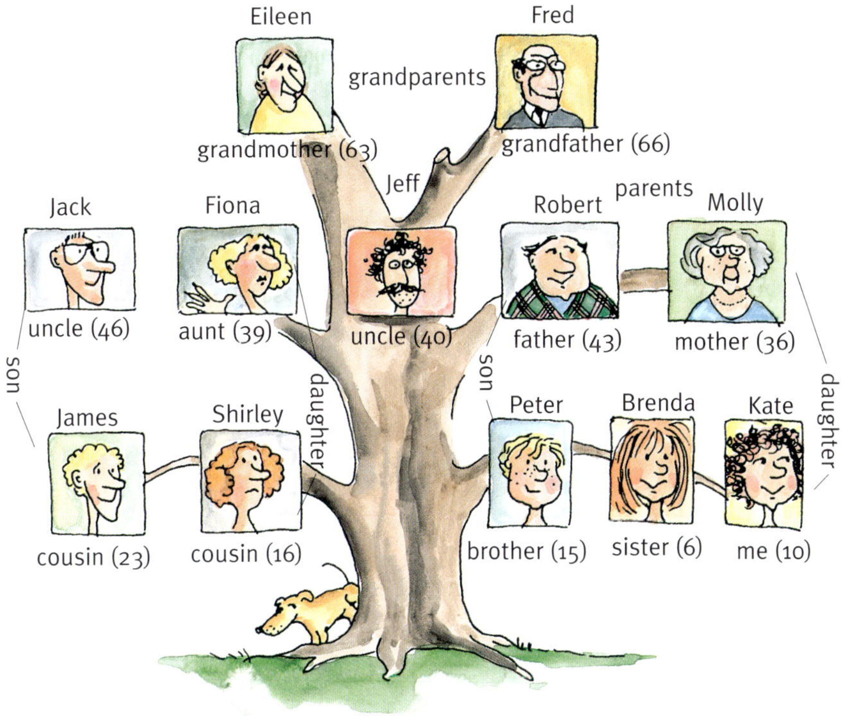

family tree – Stammbaum

12.5 Who are they?

Complete the sentences.

Sieh dir den Stammbaum an und trage die Verwandtschaftsbezeichnungen ein.

Robert is my father.

Fred is my ....

Jack is my ....

James is my ....

Fiona is my ....

Brenda is my ....

Eileen is my ....

Peter is my ....

Molly is my ....

Shirley is my ....

12.6 A family crossword puzzle

Fill in the missing words.

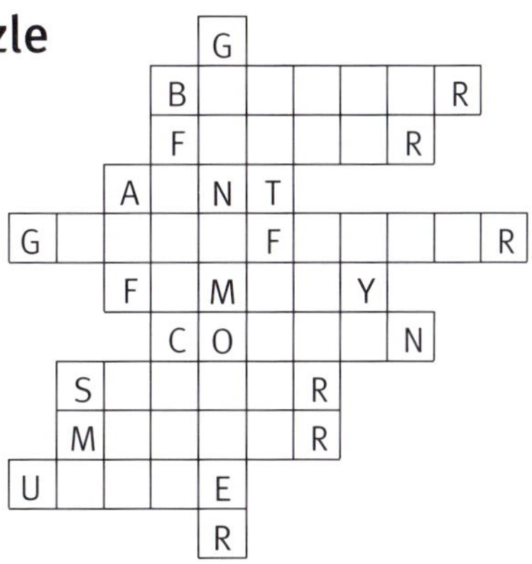

12.7 Matching exercise

relatives – Verwandte

Your family	relatives
A Your mother's sister is your ...	1 grandfather
B Your sister is your parents' ...	2 aunt
C Your aunt is your mother's ...	3 grandmother
D Your parents' daughter is your ...	4 mother
E Your (girl) cousin is your uncle's ...	5 daughter
F Your father's wife is your ...	6 aunt
G What do you call your father's sister?	7 daughter
H What do you call your mother's mother?	8 sister
I Your uncle's father is your ...	9 sister

Complete the sentences.

A	2	Your mother's sister is your aunt.
B		....
C		....
D		....
E		....
F		....
G		....
H		....
I		....

12.8 The Case family

Kate stellt ihre Familie vor.

Kate introduces her family. Fill in the missing personal pronouns (I, he, she, it, we, they)

This is me, Kate.

...I...'m 10 years old. This is Brenda, my little sister. .... is 6. This is my father. .... is 43 years old and this is my mother. .... is 36. .... are my parents. This is Peter, my elder brother. .... is 15. This is Benny the dog. .... is my sister's dog. Here are my father's sister Fiona and her husband Jack. .... are my aunt and uncle and they are very nice. Most of all .... like my father's mum and dad, my grandparents. .... give me extra pocket money. .... are really kind.

husband – Ehemann

12.9 A conversation

Dialogue

Complete the conversation between Kate and Robin.
Fill in the personal pronouns (I, you, he, she, they).

Vervollständige das Gespräch zwischen Kate und Robin.

Robin: Hello, Kate!
How are .... ?
Kate: Fine, thanks.
Robin: Have .... got any brothers and sisters?
Kate: Yes, ... have.
Robin: How many have .... got?
Kate: One brother and one sister.
Robin: I see, how old are .... ?
Kate: My brother Peter, ... is fifteen and my sister Brenda, ... is six. Have .... got any brothers and sisters?
Robin: Yes, ... have. .... 've got one brother.
Kate: How old is .... ?
Robin: .... is one.

12.10 Over to you: My family tree

Look at page 59. Fill in the names of the members of your family.

13. Demonstrative Pronouns/ Demonstrativpronomen

Grammar

Das hinweisende Fürwort gebraucht man, wenn man auf etwas zeigt. Der Unterschied liegt in der Entfernung, die du zu dem Gegenstand hast, auf den du hinweist.

This	*here*	zeigt auf etwas im Singular, das ganz nahe ist.

This is a book.

That	*over there*	zeigt auf etwas im Singular, das weiter entfernt ist.

That is a book.

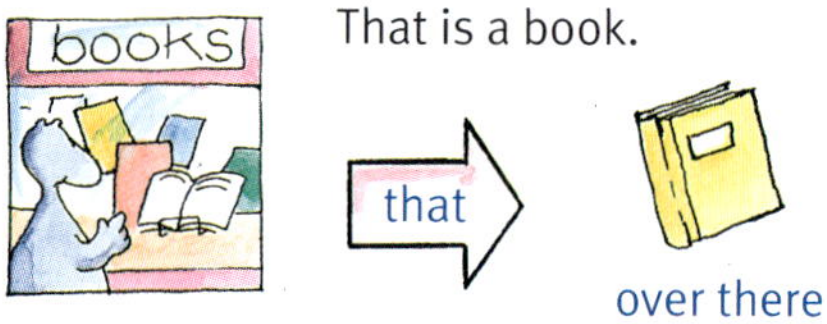

this *that*	*he* *she* *it*	*this / that* gebraucht man, wenn man über die 3. Person Singular spricht.

These sagt man, wenn man auf etwas im Plural zeigt, das in der Nähe ist.

These are my books.

Those sagt man, wenn man auf mehrere Gegenstände zeigt, die weiter entfernt sind.

Those are my books.

these *those*	*they*	*these / those* gebraucht man, wenn man über die 3. Person Plural spricht.

13.1 Fred's questions

Fill in!

This or these?

This .... is milk.
.... are cups.
.... are oranges.
.... is a spoon.
.... is a fork.
.... are plates.
.... is honey.

That or those?

That .... is tea.
.... are plates.
.... are bags.
.... are eggs.
.... is a horse show.
.... is an apple tree.
.... are lemons.

13.2 Questions and answers

Are these your cats?
Yes, they are.

....?
No, they are Peter's.

....?
No, it's Karen's.

....?
No, it's Mum's.

....?
No, ...
Mr. Peabody's.

....?
No, ...
Kim's.

....?
Yes, it is.

....?
No, ...
Susan's.

....?
Yes, ...

....?
No, ...
Brenda's.

14. The Verb *to be* (Present Tense)/ Das Verb „sein“ im Präsens

Grammar

Die Formen von *to be*

Die Formen von ***to be*** werden meistens verkürzt, besonders beim Sprechen. Bei den Kurzformen wird ein Buchstabe ausgelassen. Dafür bleibt ein Apostroph **’** stehen.

	Long forms	Short forms
	I am	I’m
	you are	you’re
	he is	he’s
	she is	she’s
	it is	it’s
	we are	we’re
	you are	you’re
	they are	they’re

14.1 Do you know the Case family?

Look at the family tree on page 65 and write.

I am  I am a girl.
My name is Kate.

 I .... a ....
My name ....

You are Draw your face in the mirror. 

You .... a ....
Your name ....

He is
She is

She .... my sister.
He ....

It is

What is it?

It .... a ....

We are

We .... the Case family.

You are

You ....
my brother
and sister.

They are

They .... my family.

14.2 Filling in exercise

Fill in the correct forms of to be.

1. Henry ....is.... a student.
2. He .... a good teacher.
3. We .... busy.
4. You and Sarah .... sisters.
5. The door .... closed.
6. I .... tired now.
7. This .... a good exercise.
8. Mr. and Mrs. Ashing .... English.
9. We .... brothers.
10. I .... happy.
11. You .... a good student.
12. She .... a good friend.
13. Karen and I .... good friends.

busy – beschäftigt

Hide and seek – Verstecken spielen

14.3 Hide and seek

***Fill in* am, are, is**

It .... Saturday afternoon. Mr. and Mrs. Case .... in the garden. They .... having tea. Kate and Brenda .... there, too. Some time later Peter and Shirley .... coming. Now the children .... playing hide and seek. Kate .... counting to ten. Peter .... behind a tree. Brenda and Shirley .... in the house. Kate says, “Peter, I can’t see you. .... you up a tree?” Peter says, “No, I’.......... not. I .... behind the tree.” “Brenda and Shirley, where .... you? I can’t find you,” Kate says. Brenda and Shirley answer, “We .... here in the house.”

behind – hinter

14.4 Holiday postcards

***Here’s a postcard from Brenda. Fill in the correct form of* to be.**

to enjoy – Freude haben an

to miss – vermissen

Dear Kate,
I ______ on holiday in Soller in Majorca. Today the weather ______ fine, the wind ______ nice and cool. Swimming and surfing, enjoying the sun, I can tell you, this ______ fun. I ______ glad that there ______ no school and I ______ happy that we ______ here but my friends ______ so far away and I really miss you!

Love from Majorca,
Brenda

Frage- und Verneinungsformen von *to be*

Natürlich benutzt man Formen von ***to be*** auch in Fragesätzen und in der Verneinung. Die Formen von ***to be*** werden mit ***not*** verneint und meist werden die *short forms* benutzt. Dabei fällt das *o* von *not* weg. Dafür steht ein Auslassungszeichen: *You are not → You aren’t*
Du bildest Fragesätze mit ***to be***, indem du die Form von ***to be*** an den Anfang des Satzes stellst.
Example: ***Is*** *Julia your friend? Yes, she is.*
Are *you German? No, I am not, I am Danish.*

Grammar

Nur bei *I am* wird *not* immer in ungekürzter Form verwendet.
I am not → I’m not

Statements		Questions	Negations
Long forms	Short forms		Short forms
I am not	I’m not	Am I late?	No, you aren’t.
you are not	you aren’t	Are you ready?	No, I’m not.
he is not	he isn’t	Is he there?	No, he isn’t.
she is not	she isn’t	Is she funny?	No, she isn’t.
it is not	it isn’t	Is it cold?	No, it isn’t.
we are not	we aren’t	Are we late?	No, you aren’t.
you are not	you aren’t	Are you sisters?	No, we aren’t.
they are not	they aren’t	Are they English?	No, they aren’t.

14.5 Questions and answers

Form questions and answers. Write them in your exercise book.

Example: that / your English textbook ? – my German book
Is that your English textbook? – No, it isn’t. It’s my German book.

1. she / Kate’s mother?	the English teacher
2. I / silly?	clever
3. his name / Mike?	Peter
4. Brenda / nine?	ten
5. you Colin?	Joe
6. you / her friend?	her brother
7. that / Sue?	Peggy
8. you / from Denmark?	Germany
9. Kate / Pete’s sister?	Lee’s sister

14.6 Mixed exercise

Fill in the forms of to be.

1. My name ....is.... John.
2. I .... a boy.
3. Jenny and Ella .... sisters. They .... from London.
4. What .... your brother's name? Lee.
5. Where .... your pencils? They .... in my satchel.
6. Who .... your teacher? Mrs. Thompson.
7. How old .... you? I .... ten.
8. .... you English? No, I .... not. I .... German.
9. .... they lemons? No, they .... They .... oranges.
10. .... I on time? No, you .... You .... late.

14.7 You about yourself

Fill in the forms of to be *and answer the questions. Write them in your exercise book.*

What ..is.. your name?

What .... your address?

What .... your telephone number?

How old .... you?

.... you a boy or a girl?

What nationality .... you?

What colour .... your eyes?

What colour .... your hair?

What .... the name of your school?

What class .... you in?

14.8 Forms of the verb *to be* in the present tense

***1. Fill in the correct forms of* to be.**

I am .... a student.

Henry .... a student.

This .... a good book.

Henry and Maria .... good students.

We .... good students, too.

Mr. Smith .... a teacher.

He .... a good teacher.

You .... a good student.

Helen and Maria .... good students.

They .... sisters.

I .... very busy today.

Henry .... busy today, too.

2. Change to negative.

Verneine die Sätze.

We are brothers. We aren't brothers.

Today is Monday. ....

I am a good student. ....

John and I are in the same class. ....

This is a good exercise. ....

The door is closed. ....

We are friends. ....

You and George are good friends. ....

I am German. ....

3. Change into questions.

Wandle in Fragesätze um.

They are brothers. Are they brothers?

Miss Jones is a good teacher. ....

I am happy today. ....

We are going to school now. ....

Mr. and Mrs. Ashing are English. ....

Your father is 42. ....

Your sisters are 12 and 16. ....

This is Sarah. ....

15. The Verb *to have got* / Das Verb „haben“

Grammar

Das Verb ***to have got*** entspricht dem deutschen Verb „haben / besitzen“. Außer bei der **3. Person Singular *(has got)*** steht bei allen Personen die Form ***have got***.

!

Die **Kurzformen *he's got / she's got*** und ***it's got*** werden **leicht** mit den **Kurzformen *he's*** *(he is)*, ***she's*** *(she is)* und ***it's*** *(it is)* **verwechselt**.

	Long forms	
I	have got	a box
you	have got	
he/she/it	has got	
we	have got	
you	have got	
they	have got	

	Short forms	
I	've got	a box
you	've got	
he/she/it	's got	
we	've got	
you	've got	
they	've got	

15.1 They have got a lot of things

Write down what Patty and her classmates have got.

Has Patty got an exercise book?

Yes, she has.

Has Bob got a pencil?

No, he hasn't. He's got a pen.

Has Joe got a pencil case?

....

Have Susan and Peter got an English book?

....

Have Betty and Paul got a biro?

....

Has Simon got a ruler?

....

Verneinende Formen

Wenn man die Aussagen mit ***have / has got*** verneinen möchte, fügt man ***not*** zwischen ***have / has*** und ***got*** ein.

Grammar

	Long forms	
I you he/she/it	have not got have not got has not got	a box
we you they	have not got have not got have not got	

	Short forms	
I you he/she/it	haven't got haven't got hasn't got	a box
we you they	haven't got haven't got haven't got	

15.2 What have they got and what not?

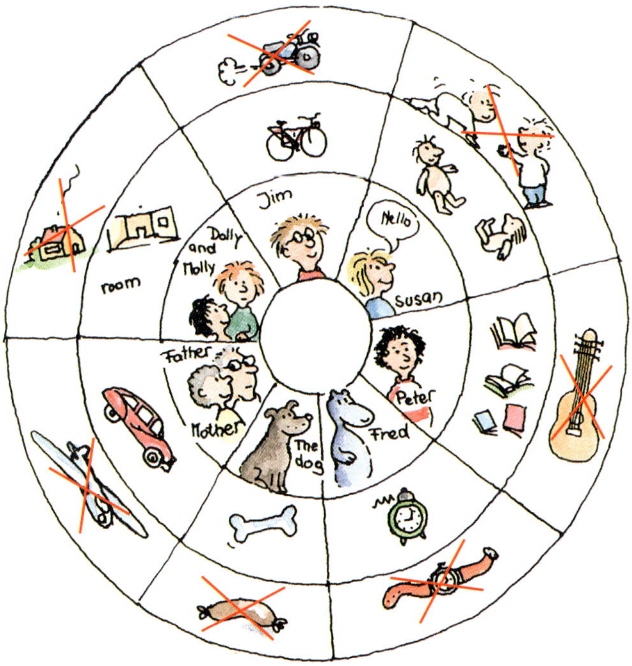

Example: **Jim** has got a bike **but** he hasn't got a motorbike.

Susan .... but ....

Peter .... but ....

Fred .... but ....

The dog .... but ....

My father and mother .... but they ....

Dolly and Molly .... but ....

Grammar

Fragesätze mit *have / has got*

Du bildest Fragesätze mit ***have / has got***, indem du ***have / has*** an den **Anfang des Satzes** und ***got*** zwischen **Subjekt** und **Objekt** stellst.
Have you got a bike?
Bei Kurzantworten musst du das ***got*** wegfallen lassen.
*Has she got a nice name? Yes, she **has** / No, she **hasn't**.*

Question	Long forms/short forms
Have I got a good job? Have I got a nice name? Have you got a dog? Has he / she / it got a garden?	Yes, you have. No, you haven't. Yes, I have. No, I haven't. Yes, he / she / it has. No, he / she / it hasn't.
Have we got a bike? Have you got your keys? Have your friends got a cassette recorder?	Yes, we have. No, we haven't. Yes, we have. No, we haven't. Yes, they have. No, they haven't.

15.3 Interviewing people

Look at the picture and answer the questions.

1. Has Trish got a piece of chalk? Yes, she has.
2. Has Sally got three teddy bears? No, she hasn't.
3. Has Trish got an English book? ....
4. Has Nick got five balls? ....
5. Has Sally got two calculators? ....
6. Has Nick got four birds? ....
7. Has Trish got a schoolbag? ....
8. Has Sally got a bike? ....

15.4 How many have they got?

Bob and Patrick are brothers. Look at their bedroom and ask questions about what they have got and what not.

Formuliere Fragen und Antworten. Sieh dir auch das Kapitel 10 über die Pluralbildung noch einmal an.

5 toy cars / 2 schoolbags / 3 chairs / 4 hats / 6 posters / 10 apples / 3 lamps / 2 tables / 2 teddy bears / 4 flags / 5 dolls / 6 books

Example:

5 toy cars	Have you got five toy cars? No, we haven't. We have got seven.
2 schoolbags	Have you got two schoolbags? Yes, we have.
3 chairs	....? No, we haven't. We ....
4 hats	....? ....
6 posters	....? ....

Continue in your exercise book.

15.5 A mindmap

Write satellites and say what you have got.

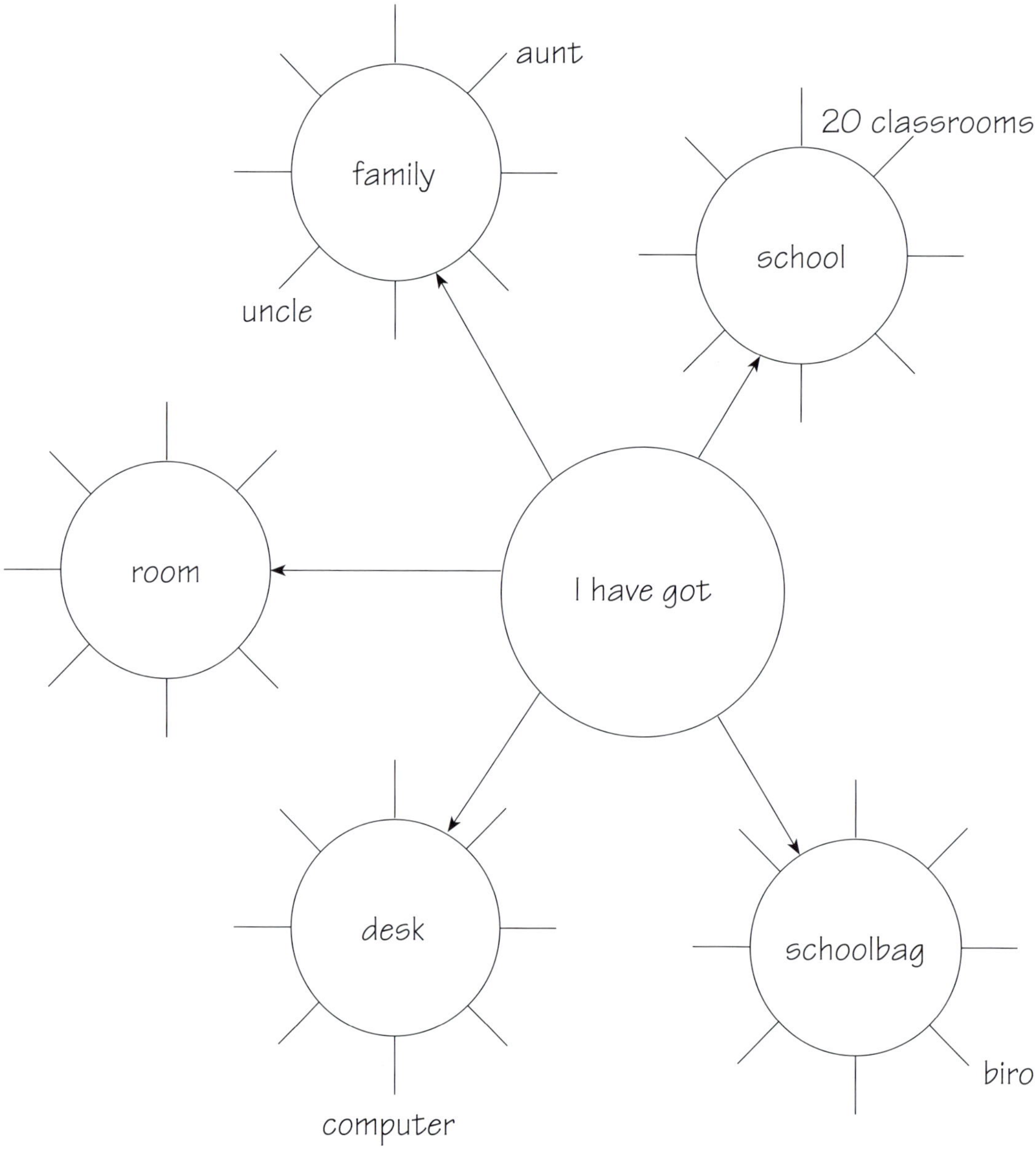

Family: I have got two aunts and one uncle, ...

School: My school has got 20 classrooms, ...

Room: My room has got a computer, ...

Schoolbag: In my schoolbag I have got ....

Desk: On my desk I have got ....

16. Pets

Words

puppy – Welpe, junger Hund

16.1 What pets have they got?

Susan has got .... Aunt Lily has got ....

Words

Pets: Parts of the body

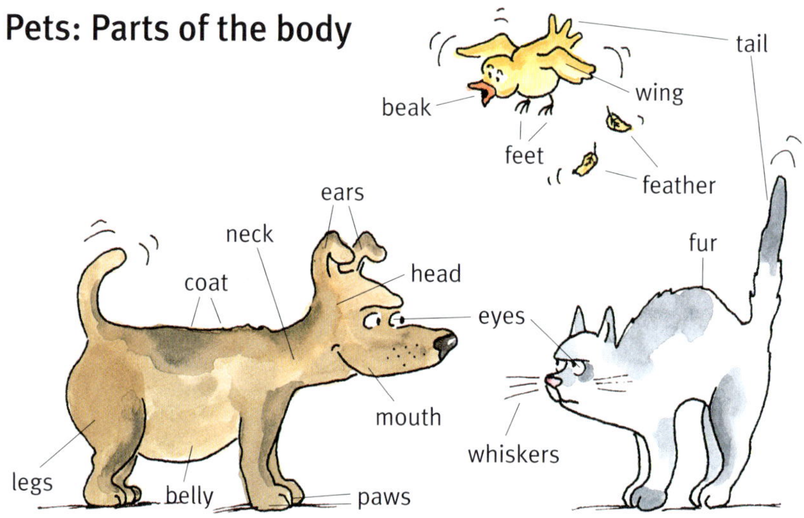

16.2 What have the pets got?

1. The dog has got four paws.

2. The squirrel has got a long ....

3. The parrot has got colourful ....

4. This rabbit has got long ....

5. This canary has got a yellow ....

6. This cat has got black and white ....

7. The tortoise has got four ....

16.3 Children and their pets

has got	sleeps	drinks/eats	feeds	
Peter 	 in the kitchen	water, bones, meat, ... 	before he does his home-work	 barks very loudly
Jill 	 in a basket in her bedroom	milk, fish, meat, ... 	in the afternoon	 catches mice and birds
Sally 	 in a cage	food from the pet shop, water 	before she goes to bed	 sleeps during the day, is active during the night
Sarah 	 in a bowl	fish food 	in the morning	 is boring
Kevin 	 in a cage	birdseed 	when he comes home from school	 is very noisy

boring – langweilig

noise – Lärm

Answer the questions.

1. Who has got a budgie?
2. Where does the cat sleep?
3. What does a goldfish eat?
4. What does a cat drink?
5. Who feeds Sally's hamster?
6. When does Peter feed his dog?

budgie – Wellensittich

Write sentences about the children.

Peter has got a dog. Peter's dog sleeps in the kitchen. It drinks water and eats bones and meat. Peter feeds his dog before he does his homework. His dog barks very loudly.

Go on with Jill / Sally / Sarah and Kevin. Write in your exercise book.

16.4 Keeping a pet

Ordne die Satzhälften zu und schreibe die Sätze in dein Heft.

Match the halves and write the sentences in your exercise book.

If you want a hamster,
If you want to forget your pet in the winter,
If you want to keep a cat,
If you want to keep a goldfish,
If you want to keep a mouse,
If you want to keep a dog,
If you want to keep a rabbit,

don't forget it sometimes brings you dead mice and birds.
you must clean its hutch out twice a week and brush it with a small brush.
you must take it for a long walk every day.
get a tortoise.
don't forget it is active at night and it sometimes bites.
don't forget it smells a bit.
don't put the fish tank in direct sunlight.

to keep – halten

to smell – riechen

Example:

If you want a hamster, don't forget it is active at night and it sometimes bites.

Reading

16.5 Talking about pets

Susan and Jerry are talking about pets. Here is what they say. Read aloud.

We've got a pet, a dog. His name is Toby. He is about three years old. When I come home he wags his tail. Then I play with him in the garden because he needs a lot of exercise. He has got a black nose, brown eyes and a white tail. His ears are black and his paws are brown. He knows a lot of tricks. He can play catch and he can use his nose to play football. He sleeps in our kitchen in a basket. I have to clean it twice a week. When I have a lot of homework to do my father looks after our dog but mostly I do.

I haven't got a pet, but I'd like to have one, a cat. My parents won't let me have a pet. Our flat is too small.

16.6 Susan and her pet

Dialogue

Now talk to Susan about her pet.

You

Have you got a pet?

Susan

Yes, I have a dog.

He has a black nose, brown eyes and a white tail.

He's about three years old.

His name is Toby.

Yes, I play with him in the garden.

No, not really. I clean the basket twice a week.

My father does when I have a lot of homework.

What about you? Have you got a pet?

16.7 In a pet shop

Describe the pet shop. How many pets can you see and where are they? Write sentences in your exercise book.

There are three goldfish in a tank. Five mice are in a cage.

Dialogue

16.8 Over to you: Me and my pet

Talk about your pet / your friend's pet.

Trage die Fakten zuerst in die Vorlage ein. Schreibe dann einen zusammenhängenden Text.

My pet is a ....

name: ....

what	he	eats: ....
what	she	drinks: ....
what		likes: ....

My dream pet is a ....

name: ....

what he / she eats: ....

what he / she drinks: ....

what he / she likes: ....

I've (We've) got a ....

(dog / cat / rabbit / guinea pig / budgie / hamster / tortoise / goldfish)

I haven't got a pet, but my friend has got a pet.

He / She has got ....

His / Her name is ....

What colour is he / she? ....

lazy – faul

hut – Hütte

Is he / she funny / clever / fast / stupid / lazy?

Has he / she got a cage / a basket / a hut?

Where does he / she live?

He / She lives in the garden / in the kitchen / in the living room / in my room.

17. The Present Progressive Form / Die Verlaufsform der Gegenwart

Mit dem *present progressive* drückt man aus, dass jemand gerade etwas tut oder dass ein Vorgang noch im Gange ist.

In der deutschen Sprache gibt es keine Verlaufsform. Die Bedeutung dieser Form wird im Deutschen oft mithilfe von **gerade, jetzt, im Moment** ausgedrückt.

Das *present progressive* wird gebildet mit
- einer Form von ***to be*** in der Gegenwart: ***am / are / is / are*** (die Formen findest du auf Seite 64 ff.)
- **und** der Grundform des Verbs + ***ing***: ***work*** + ***ing*** → ***working***

Grammar

Long forms

I	am	playing
you	are	playing
he	is	playing
she	is	playing
it	is	playing
we	are	playing
you	are	playing
they	are	playing

Short forms

I	'm	playing
you	're	playing
he	's	playing
she	's	playing
it	's	playing
we	're	playing
you	're	playing
they	're	playing

17.1 Look at the animals

What are they doing? Fill in.

1. The budgie (sing) .... in the cage.
2. The tortoise (look) .... at the bird.
3. The fish (dream) .... about the ocean.
4. The dog (wait) .... for his food.
5. The cat (sleep) .... in the basket.
6. The mouse (make) .... fun of the cat.

to make fun of – sich lustig machen über

17.2 What are the people doing?

Here are some pictures.

Fill in.

1. Daddy (cook) is cooking .... our meal.
2. Thomas (play) .... football.
3. The cat (jump) .... on the table.
4. Jim (do) .... his homework.
5. Mandy (watch) .... TV.
6. Tanja (read) .... a book.
7. Julia (ride) .... her bike.
8. Peter (look) .... out of the window.
9. Mummy (clean) .... the window.
10. Maria (pick) .... flowers.

17.3 Questions

Now let's ask the people what they are doing.

1. Daddy, what are you doing? I am cooking .... our meal.
2. Thomas, what ....? I .... football.
3. Cat, what are you doing? I .... on the table.
4. Jim, ...? .... homework.
5. Mandy, ...? .... television.
6. Tanja, ...? .... reading a book.
7. Julia, ...? I .... bike.
8. Peter, ...? .... window.
9. Mummy, what are you doing? .... the window.
10. Maria, what are you doing? .... flowers.

Besonderheiten der Schreibung

Wie das *present progressive* im Normalfall gebildet wird, weißt du ja schon. Allerdings gibt es drei Besonderheiten, welche die Schreibweise betreffen.

1. Ein stummes -e am Ende der Verben fällt weg:
smile + ing → smiling *close + ing → closing*

2. Der Konsonant nach kurzem Vokal wird verdoppelt:
cut + ing → cutting *drop + ing → dropping*

3. Aus -ie am Ende des Verbes wird -y:
lie + ing → lying

Grammar

17.4 Progressive Forms

Fill in the progressive forms of the verbs.

Bilde aus den Verben die progressive form und schreibe sie auf die vorgesehenen Linien.

1. closing
2. ....
3. ....
4. ....
5. ....
6. ....
7. ....
8. ....
9. ....
10. ....
11. ....
12. ....
13. ....
14. ....
15. ....
16. ....
17. ....

6. take 12. get
17. lie 5. sit
9. swim 3. smoke
1. close 16. put
13. eat 15. hide
10. make 8. cut
2. write 14. dance
7. read 11. shut
4. play

17.5 What is happening at the moment?

Fill in the correct forms of the verbs.

1. Fred is reading (read) a book.
2. We .... (have) our English lesson now.
3. Daddy is busy now. He .... (write) a letter.
4. Brenda .... (swim) in the pool at the moment.
5. Sarah .... (phone) her boyfriend.
6. Daddy .... (smoke) his pipe.
7. The cat .... (run) after the mouse.
8. They .... (get) on the bus.
9. Fred .... (lie) on the floor.
10. The girls .... (sit) in the garden.
11. The teacher .... (close) the window in the classroom.

17.6 What are they doing?

Write sentences. Use the verbs in the box. Write them in your exercise book.

read (2x) – wash (2x) – swim – sit (2x) – play (4x) – count – sing (2x) – brush – look – sleep – write (2x) – bark – paint – stand – listen to – watch

Example

1. The boy is writing a letter.

17·7 Peter's day

Find out what he is doing. Write in your exercise book.

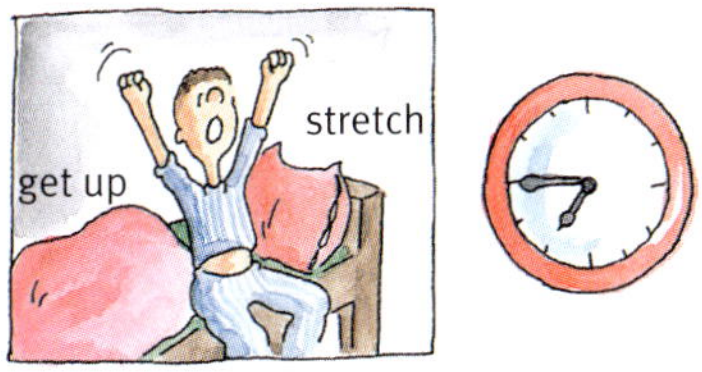

It's .... Peter is in bed.
He ....
He .... his arms.

It's .... now. Peter ....
a glass of milk. His sister .... an
apple, his mother .... cornflakes.
His father .... a newspaper.

It's .... Peter and his sister
.... at the bus stop.
They .... for the bus.

It's .... The teacher ....
in front of the class. Peter ....
from a book. The other pupils ....
on their chairs and ....
in their exercise books.

It's .... now. Peter ....
football with his friends in the play-
ground. A dog .... loudly.

It's .... Peter and his sister
.... home. They ....
on a bus. Three boys ....
to the bus stop.

It's .... Peter .... on
the floor and .... TV. His
father and mother .... on
the sofa and .... cards.
Peter's sister .... a book.

Grammar

Signalwörter

Das *present progressive* kommt oft mit bestimmten Wörtern vor, die darauf hinweisen, dass eine Handlung gerade abläuft.

Man sagt, sie signalisieren die Zeit.

Solche **Signalwörter** für das *present progressive* sind:

just → gerade / ***just now*** → gerade jetzt / ***still*** → immer noch / ***at the (this) moment*** → im Augenblick / ***look*** → schau! / ***listen*** → hör hin (zu)

17.8 Signals

Fill in the correct form of the verb.

Listen! The train .... (come).

Look! The dog .... (chase) the cat.

Daddy .... (cook) our meal at the moment.

The girls .... just .... (go) to the birthday party.

The bird .... still .... (sit) on the roof.

I .... (do) my homework just now.

Listen! Somebody .... (come) up the stairs.

Look! Mummy .... (smile) at the baby.

Peter .... still (do) his homework.

I .... (take) the dog out at the moment.

17.9 Mrs. Jackson is absent

What is happening in the classroom at the moment?

Mrs. Jackson, the English teacher, usually comes into the classroom at 11.30. But today she isn't at school, and so the pupils (have) are having .... a nice time. Two boys (play) .... football with a coke bottle. Simon (draw) .... a funny man on the board. It's a picture of Mr. Teabody, the biology teacher at this school. Jack and Cathy (write) .... their names on the window-pane with a felt pen. They love each other very much. A lot of the girls (do) .... their homework now. Some of the boys (look) .... out of the window. They (watch) .... other pupils playing football. Billy and Tom (stand) .... on the desks. At this moment Mr. Teabody (come) .... into the classroom. He (carry) .... books. He is very angry about the noise in the classroom.

pane – Scheibe

18. The Auxiliary *can* / Das Hilfsverb „können“

18.1 Spare time activities

Match the activities below to the pictures. Write under the pictures.

1 ....

2 ....

3 ....

4 ....

5 ....

6 ....

7 ....

8 ....

9 ....

10 ....

11 ....

12 ....

play football – ride a bike – fish – skate – ski – swim – sail – dance – play tennis – organise his stamps – climb trees – ride a horse

Now write down in your exercise book what Fred can do.

Example:
Fred can play football.

Das Hilfsverb *can* drückt eine Fähigkeit oder Unfähigkeit aus. Es hat nur eine Form für alle Personen und kann nicht alleine stehen. Man muss immer ein Verb im Infinitiv (Grundform)hinzufügen, außer bei den Kurzantworten. Die verneinte Form heißt *cannot* oder kurz *can't*.

Grammar

Positive Statement

I You He/She/It	can	swim
We You They		

Negation

I You He/She/It	cannot can't	swim
We You They		

18.2 Fred's broken arm

Fred has broken his arm. Which things do you think he can and which things can't he do?

climb trees – wash his ears – go to school – open bottles – go to bed – do his homework – take a shower – use his computer – eat with a spoon – go out for a walk – play the guitar –

spoon – Löffel

Example:

Fred can't climb trees with his broken arm.
Fred can go out for a walk.

....

....

....

....

....

Go on in your exercise book.

18.3 Animals

Describe what the animals can do or can't do. Write in your exercise book.

fly – swim – run fast – jump – hear well – pull carts – climb trees – sing – see well – smell very well – catch mice – eat other animals – live without water – eat bananas – bark

Example: Rabbits can run very fast but they can't see very well.

18.4 I'm thinking of an animal

Du kennst doch das Spiel? Einer denkt sich ein Tier und der andere versucht es durch Fragen zu erraten. (Bob denkt an einen Hund)

Bob is thinking of an animal (a dog) and Ann has to guess it. Fill in the gaps and finish the dialogue.

Bob: I'm thinking of an animal.
Ann: Can it climb trees, Bob?
Bob: No, it can't.

Ann: .... it fly?

Bob: No, ...

Ann: .... it walk on two legs?

Bob: No, ...

Ann: .... it hear well?

Bob: Yes, ...

Go on in your exercise book.

18.5 Things you can do – things you can't do

Write sentences in your exercise book.

Example:
I can swim but I can't walk on my hands.

18.6 Over to you: Rules at home

rules – Regeln

Answer the questions.

Can you go out whenever you want?	I have to ask my parents first. I can only go out at the weekend. I can only go out after I have done my homework. ...
When you go out, can you go where you want?	I can only go out if my parents know where I'm going. I can only go to people my parents know. I can only go out with friends my parents know. I can't go to the cinema. ...
What time do you have to be home?	I have to be home by ten o'clock. I can come home whenever I want. ...
What happens if you come home late?	My parents are angry if I come home late. If I come home late, I don't get any pocket money. ...

19. Simple Present Tense / Das einfache Präsens

Grammar

Der Gebrauch des Simple Presents

Das *simple present* wird bei Tätigkeits- und Vorgangsverben benutzt,

1. wenn etwas wiederholt wird oder immer wieder passiert. Hier geht es um Gewohnheiten.
   My father gets up at six every morning.
   I always play tennis on Wednesdays.
2. wenn etwas immer so ist. Hier geht es um allgemeine Tatsachen.
   The sun rises in the east.
   The Thames flows into the North Sea.
3. wenn Handlungen aufeinander folgen. Du findest diese Form bei Erzählungen, Sportberichten und Gebrauchsanweisungen.
   Shirley wakes up, yawns, stretches her arms, gets out of bed and goes to the bathroom.

In der 3. Person Singular musst du an das Verb ein s hängen. Merke dir: He, she, it, das s muss mit.

Sally – she –
Peter – he –
the cat – it

to the station

I – you –
we – they

the room

19.1 Forms of the verbs in the present tense

Choose the correct form of the verb. Write the sentences into your exercise book.

1. Harry's parents (get, gets) up at seven o'clock every day.
2. They all (have, has) breakfast in the kitchen.
3. He (go, goes) to school by bus.
4. They (live, lives) in the country.
5. Harry's mother (is, are) a teacher.
6. They (come, comes) home at four o'clock.
7. In the afternoon Harry often (play, plays) football with his friends.
8. He (listen, listens) to pop music.
9. He (like, likes) pop music.
10. In the evening they (watch, watches) television.

Besonderheiten der Schreibung

1. Im Normalfall wird an die Grundform des Verbs ein **-s** angehängt:
   to ask – he asks
   to write – she writes
   to happen – it happens
2. Endet das Verb auf einen **Zischlaut**, so wird **-es** angehängt:
   to watch – he watches
   to fetch – he fetches
   to miss – it misses
3. Endet das Verb auf **Konsonant und -y**, dann wird -y zu **-ie** und ein **-s** angehängt:
   to fly – it flies
   to hurry – she hurries
4. Endet das Verb auf **Vokal und -y**, dann bleibt das -y und es wird einfach ein **-s** angehängt:
   to play – she plays
   to say – he says

Ausnahme: *I go – he goes* *I do – he does*

Grammar

19.2 The 3rd person singular verb machine

Fill in the correct forms.

1. you say ... he / she says
2. they fly ...
3. we get ...
4. I fetch ...
5. you do ...
6. I buy ...
7. they catch ...
8. we cook ...
9. you hurry ...
10. I go ...
11. you kiss ...

Fred writes.

19.3 European children

Write sentences about the children.

	Katrin	Mustafa	Sven	Paula
to live	Munich	Hamburg	Oslo	Madrid
to come from	Germany	Turkey	Norway	Spain
to speak	German English	Turkish German	Norwegian German	Spanish English
to play	table tennis	football	volleyball	tennis
to collect	stickers	CDs	comics	posters
to like	sweets	dancing	swimming	riding
to hate	gardening	maths	eggs	spinach

Example: Katrin lives in Munich. She comes from Germany and speaks German and English. She plays table tennis and collects stickers. She likes sweets and hates gardening.

19.4 A gentleman

What can you say about this gentleman? Write down sentences.

name	David	30	to be 30 years old
to live in	London	GB	to come from
to live in	flat	4 rooms	to have 4 rooms
to work as a	teacher	big school	to work in a
to speak	English	German	to speak
to be	married	2 children	to have
to like	football	Italy	
	fishing	boxing	
		TV	to hate
to play	tennis	beer	
		warm milk	
to collect	stamps		
	records		

Example: His name is David. He is thirty years old.

Signalwörter

Folgende Signalwörter zeigen dir an, dass du *simple present tense* verwenden musst:

1. Für Tätigkeiten und Vorgänge, die sich wiederholen oder immer wieder passieren:

often	oft	*every day*	jeden Tag
always	immer	*never*	niemals
sometimes	manchmal	*usually*	gewöhnlich
seldom	selten		

2. Für Handlungen, die aufeinander folgen:

first	zuerst	*lastly*	zum Schluss
then	dann	*finally*	zum Schluss
after that	danach		

Grammar

19.5 What do you do?

Write sentences about the children and about yourself.

	Fred	Daniel	Peter	You
listen to CDs	sometimes with friends	never on Mondays	every day	
read books	often	sometimes	seldom	
play football	often	never	never	
do house-work	never	seldom	every day	
watch TV	usually in the evening	sometimes pop shows	often action movies	

Example: Fred sometimes listens to CDs with friends.

Continue in your exercise book.

19.6 Jobs at home

Look at the pictures and write down in your exercise book what Fred does at home.

do the cooking – wash the dishes – clean the floor – do the shopping – wash the car – set the table – water the flowers – clean the shoes – make breakfast – empty the dustbin – make the beds – wash the clothes – tidy the bedroom

Examples:

Fred waters the flowers.
Fred does the cooking.
...

19.7 Over to you: Family jobs

Write down in your exercise book how often you and the members of your family do these jobs.

I	never	do(es)	the cooking
My	sometimes		the washing-up
– mother	often		the shopping
– father	usually	wash(es)	the car
– brother	seldom	lay(s)	the table
– sister	always	clean(s)	the shoes
		repair(s)	broken things

19.8 Waking up in the morning

Write down how Fred wakes the boy up. Write in your exercise book. Use the following signal words:

first – then – after that – finally

This list will help you:

offer sausage – hen lay an egg – sleeping boy wake up – wag tail – make hole in fish tank– bell ring – egg fall into net – water pour down – gun fire

to offer – anbieten
to pour – gießen / strömen
hole – Loch

Example: First Fred offers a sausage to his dog.

19.9 Getting up in the morning

What does Fred do every morning? Match the morning activities to the pictures and write them down in the right order.

Every morning Fred gets up at seven o'clock [1]. Then Fred goes into the bathroom ☐. Then he has a shower ☐. He washes his hands and his face ☐. Fred stretches his arms ☐. He gets out of bed ☐. After that he dries his body with a towel ☐. He puts on his shirts and his pants ☐. He rubs his eyes ☐. Finally Fred leaves the house and goes to the bus stop ☐. Then he goes downstairs to the kitchen ☐. There he sits down at the breakfast table and has breakfast ☐.

to stretch – strecken
towel – Handtuch

Grammar

Simple Present – Present Progressive

Neben dem ***simple present*** hast du bereits das ***present progressive*** kennen gelernt. Hier findest du eine Gegenüberstellung der beiden Zeiten.

	Simple Present	Present Progressive
Bildung	Personalpronomen **und** Verb in Grundform, in der 3. Person Singular kommt ein **s** an das Verb: ***I sing.*** ***He sings.***	Personalpronomen **und** eine Form von ***to be (am, is, are)*** **und** die Endung **-ing** ***I am singing.*** ***He is singing.***
Verwendung	– wenn etwas wiederholt wird oder immer passiert – wenn etwas immer so ist – wenn Handlungen aufeinander folgen	wenn eine Handlung gerade passiert
Signalwörter	Für Tätigkeiten und Vorgänge, die sich wiederholen oder immer wieder passieren: *often, always, sometimes, seldom, every day,* Für Handlungen, die aufeinander folgen: *first, then, after that, lastly, finally*	*look, listen, just, just now, at the moment*

19.10 Simple present or present progressive?

Fill in the verb in the correct tense.

1. Look! It .... (begin) to rain.
2. We .... (have) English now.
3. Mr. Evans .... (laugh) very much.
4. The bus always .... (stop) at this corner.
5. We .... (have) English four times a week.
6. It is 8 o' clock. The bus .... (come).

19.11 A fairy tale

Reading

Lies das Märchen sorgfältig durch, denn wir stellen dir einige Aufgaben dazu.

Cinderella

Cinderella has no mother. She lives with her evil stepmother and two evil stepsisters. Her sisters hate her because Cinderella is a beautiful girl and they are very ugly. Cinderella has to do all the work in the house. Her sisters don't help her.
One day the prince holds a big ball at his castle. The ugly sisters are going to the ball. Cinderella has to help them put on their beautiful dresses. Cinderella can't go to the ball. She has got no dress and no shoes. She is very unhappy and starts to cry bitterly.
Suddenly a good fairy appears. She says, "Don't cry, Cinderella! Do you want to go to the ball?"
"I'd like to go," says Cinderella, "but I can't. I have got no dress and no shoes." "I'll help you," says the fairy.
"Of course you can go to the ball. Here is a beautiful dress and a pair of shoes made of silk."
Then a coach with six horses takes her to the castle. But she has to be back home by midnight.
Cinderella is very happy. She meets the prince at the ball. They dance and dance all night. The prince falls in love with Cinderella because she is so beautiful. But then midnight comes and Cinderella has to run home. She runs away but she loses one of her shoes. The prince runs after her but he can't see her. Then he finds her shoe.
The next morning he calls his men and tells them, "Go into every house in town. Find that beautiful girl for me!" And he gives them the silk shoe. The men go into every house. Every girl tries the shoe on, but it doesn't fit. They come to Cinderella's house. Her sisters try the shoe on, but it doesn't fit.
Then Cinderella comes. She puts on the shoe and it fits. Her sisters are very angry. "You are the girl," the men say and bring her to the castle. The prince is very happy to see Cinderella. "Will you marry me?" he asks. "Yes, I will," says Cinderella. The prince marries her and they live happily ever after.

evil – böse
stepmother – Stiefmutter
ugly – hässlich
fairy – Fee
to appear – erscheinen
silk – Seide / seiden
coach – Kutsche
to marry – heiraten

19.12 Reading comprehension

„Cinderella" ist in der ganzen Welt bekannt. Hast du den englischen Text wirklich ganz genau verstanden?

Are these statements true or false? Correct the false statements and write in your exercise book.

	true	false
1. Cinderella has no mother.		
2. She has three sisters.		
3. Her sisters help her in the house.		
4. Cinderella's sisters are going to the ball.		
5. Cinderella and her sisters are going to the ball.		
6. Cinderella has got a beautiful dress but no shoes.		
7. Cinderella has got no dress and no shoes.		
8. The king and the prince hold a ball.		
9. The fairy says, "I can help you."		
10. The fairy gives Cinderella an old dress.		
11. The coach has got four horses.		
12. Cinderella sees the prince at the ball.		
13. The prince dances with Cinderella's stepmother.		
14. The prince falls in love with Cinderella.		
15. Cinderella must be home by midnight.		
16. Cinderella loses her dress.		
17. The prince finds Cinderella.		
18. The prince wants to see Cinderella.		
19. The prince goes into every house.		
20. Cinderella wants to try the shoe on.		
21. The shoe doesn't fit Cinderella.		
22. The men say to Cinderella, "You aren't the girl."		
23. They say, "Please come with us."		
24. The prince will marry one of Cinderella's sisters.		
25. The prince will marry Cinderella.		
26. They live happily ever after.		

19.13 Note taking

Take down some notes about the fairytale "Cinderella".

Time (When?)	Place (Where?)	People/Things (Who / What?)	Actions / Events / Facts (What happens?) Reasons (Why?)
	house	stepmother stepsisters Cinderella	has to do all the homework hate Cinderella
one day	castle	prince ugly sisters	holds a ball go to the ball Cinderella doesn't go hasn't got a dress
some time later	house coach	fairy Cinderella	gives Cinderella a dress goes to the ball has to be home before midnight

Go on in your exercise book.

19.14 Tell the story

Fill in the gaps.

Cinderella .... with her .... stepmother and her .... stepsisters. She is very .... because they .... her and she has to .... in the .... all day. One day the .... holds a .... at his .... The two sisters .... to the ball. Cinderella .... go. She has got no .... and no ....

Cinderella starts to .... but suddenly a .... appears. She gives Cinderella a .... and a pair of .... A coach with .... horses .... her to the .... But she must be .... at ....

Cinderella .... with the .... and they .... in love. But the prince doesn't know who she is. At 12 o'clock Cinderella .... back home and .... a silk ....

The prince tells his .... to look for the girl all over the .... Finally they find Cinderella because the shoe ....

They .... and live ....

20. Questions and Negations with *to do* / Fragen und Verneinungen mit *to do*

Reading

20.1 Answering a questionnaire

Mark your answers with a cross.

questionnaire – Fragebogen
male – männlich
female – weiblich

gathering – Treffen

relatives – Verwandte

Questionnaire – Family Life

Interviewee	Male ☐ Female ☐	Age:
Family	1. Do you live with your parents?	Yes ☐ No ☐
	2. Do you have any brothers or sisters?	Yes ☐ No ☐
Parents	3. Do your parents let you go out whenever you want?	Yes ☐ No ☐
	4. Do your parents let you go out with your friends?	Yes ☐ No ☐
	5. Do your parents usually ask you where you are going before they let you go out?	Yes ☐ No ☐
Relatives	6. Do you like big family gatherings?	Yes ☐ No ☐ Sometimes ☐
	7. Do you have a big family meal on Sundays?	Yes ☐ No ☐ Sometimes ☐
	8. Do other relatives come to see your family on Sundays?	Yes ☐ No ☐ Sometimes ☐
Homework	9. Do you have to do homework?	Yes ☐ No ☐
	10. How much time do you spend doing homework each day?	Hours: ☐
Helping at home	11. Do you have to help your mother?	Yes ☐ No ☐ Sometimes ☐
	12. Do you have to help your father?	Yes ☐ No ☐ Sometimes ☐
	13. Do you have to look after younger brothers and sisters?	Yes ☐ No ☐ Sometimes ☐
	14. Do you have to help out at the weekends?	Yes ☐ No ☐ Sometimes ☐

Now write down where you have put a cross.

Example:

I live with my parents and I have got one brother. …

Fragebildung mit *to do*

Wie du weißt, ist die Reihenfolge der Satzglieder im Englischen immer gleich:

Riders	*ride*	*horses.*
Subjekt	**Prädikat**	**Objekt**
S	P	O

Grammar

Damit diese Satzstellung auch im Fragesatz erhalten bleibt, nimmt die englische Sprache in der Gegenwart ***do*** oder ***does*** zu Hilfe. Es wird einfach an den Satzanfang gestellt.

		Subjekt	**Prädikat**	**Objekt**
Aussagesatz:		*Riders*	*ride*	*horses.*
Fragesatz:	***Do***	*riders*	*ride*	*horses?*

Das Verb ***to do*** hilft, die englische Satzstellung zu erhalten.
Dies nennt man auch Umschreibung.

!

Statement		
I You	eat	fruit.
He/She/It	eats	
We You They	eat	

Question		
Do I Do you	eat	fruit?
Does he/she/it		
Do we Do you Do they		

Umschreibung mit *to do* in der 3. Person Einzahl

Hier ist noch eine Besonderheit, die sehr wichtig ist! Das **-s** der 3. Person wandert bei der Umschreibung mit ***to do*** an den Anfang des Satzes. Aus ***do*** wird dann ***does***. Das **Verb** selbst steht immer in der **Grundform** und hat dann nie eine Endung **-s** der 3. Person.

		Subjekt	**Prädikat**	**Objekt**
Aussagesatz:		*Sarah*	*helps*	*Tom.*
Fragesatz:	*Does*	*Sarah*	*help*	*Tom?*

He, she, it –
ein **s** muss mit.
Doch steht das Wörtchen ***does*** im Satz,
ist für ein **weit'res s kein Platz**.

!

20.2 Questions with *does*

Ask questions and answer them.

1. Peter likes sport.

   Does .... he play football?

   Yes, he does. ....

2. Jacko is a monkey. ....

   he eat bananas? ....

3. Mrs. Black is a pilot. ....

   she fly planes? ....

4. Brenda is a pupil. .... she go to school? ....

5. John helps his mother in the kitchen. .... wash the dishes?

   ....

20.3 Mixed questions

***Ask questions with* do / does.**

1. The cat likes fish.

   Does the cat like fish? ....

2. You speak English.

   ....

3. Peter rides his bike.

   ....

4. I know my headmaster.

   ....

5. You often go to the cinema. ....
6. Teachers mark tests. ....
7. The pilot flies planes. ....
8. We play tennis every summer. ....
9. Children like sweets. ....
10. She lives on the second floor. ....
11. Fred likes dogs. ....

20.4 Mixed exercise

Ask questions and mark with a cross.

	Do	Does	Question
1. Mary gets up at a quarter to seven.	☐	☒	Does Mary get up at a quarter to seven?
2. She goes to the bathroom.	☐	☒	Does she
3. Her mother makes her breakfast.	☐	☐	
4. Her father and Jimmy come down from the bedroom.	☐	☐	
5. The dog barks in the garden.	☐	☐	
6. Jimmy opens the door and goes into the garden.	☐	☐	
7. Peter, Brenda and Susan wait at the gate.	☐	☐	
8. They all go to school.	☐	☐	
9. It snows in winter.	☐	☐	
10. Jack remembers him.	☐	☐	
11. He speaks English very clearly.	☐	☐	
12. John laughs a lot.	☐	☐	
13. We come to class on time.	☐	☐	
14. Your father plays football.	☐	☐	
15. I wash my face every morning.	☐	☐	

to remember – erinnern

Grammar

Verneinung mit *to do*

Sätze, in denen **weder** eine Form von ***to be*** **noch** ein **Hilfsverb** vorkommen, bilden die **Verneinung** mit der Umschreibung **durch *to do***. Die Verneinung wird wie bei *to be* und *have got* mit ***not*** gebildet. Auch hier gibt es Kurzformen: ***do not*** wird zu ***don't***, ***does not*** zu ***doesn't***.

	Subjekt	Prädikat	Objekt
Aussagesatz:	*Tom and Kevin*	*like*	*ice cream.*
Verneinung:	*Maria and Brenda*	*do not (don't) like*	*ice cream.*

Wie bei der umschriebenen Frage wandert auch bei der Verneinung das **-s** des Verbs bei der 3. Person Singular zum ***do***. Es wird dann zu ***does***.

Example:
Tom likes potatoes.
Verneinung: *Tom does not (doesn't) like potatoes.*

!

Bilde **nie** die **Verneinung** eines Satzes einfach mit not, **ohne** ein **Hilfsverb** oder ***to do*** zu verwenden.

20.5 Likes and dislikes – eating and drinking

Write down sentences in your exercise book.

Example: I like juice but I don't like milk.

biscuits

juice

potatoes

toast

tomatoes

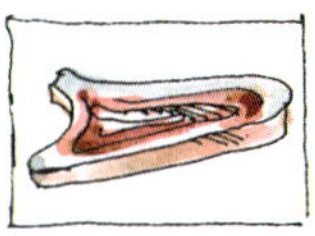
meat

onions

carrots

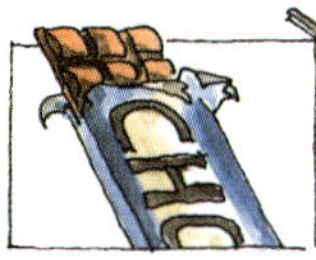
chocolate

rice

cake

milk

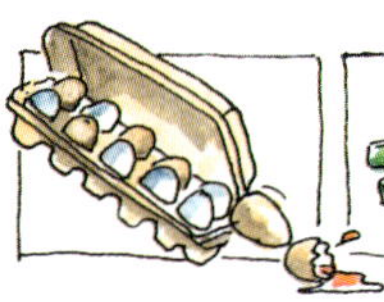
eggs

chewing gum

coffee

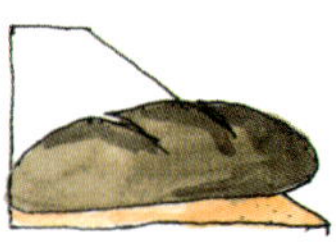
bread

water

jam

lemonade

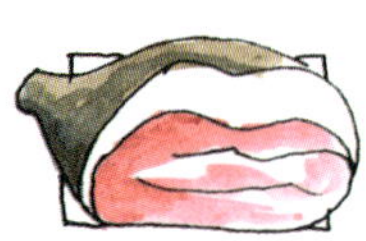
bacon

20.6 The likes and dislikes of Mr. Brown

Complete the sentences. Use the phrases below.

work – doing the washing-up – going to work – driving the car – listening to music – going out for walks – cleaning the car – drinking beer – reading the newspaper – drinking tea

\+

Mr. Brown likes drinking beer but he doesn't like ....

drinking tea. ....

–

\+

Mr. Brown likes ....

....

–

\+

....

....

–

\+

....

....

–

\+

....

....

–

20.7 Billy and Brenda are talking about school

***Fill in* do/does, don't.**

Billy: .... you like to go to school?

Brenda: Yes, I do.

Billy: .... learn English at school?

Brenda: No, ...

Brenda: .... your teacher speak German?

Billy: Yes, he ....

Billy: .... your teacher drink milk during the lesson?

Brenda: No, ...

Brenda: .... your teacher read a newspaper during lesson?

Billy: ...., he ....

Billy: .... your parents help you with your homework?

Brenda: Yes, ...

Billy: .... you and your friends like geography?

Brenda: No, ...

20.8 Over to you

What do you do and what don't you do? Write down the answers in your exercise book.

Do you live with your parents?	Do you play tennis?	Do you often go swimming in summer?	Do you know how to dance?
Do you often watch television?	Do your friends often play games with you?	Do you like school?	Do you walk to school every day?
Do you like watching football games?	Do you go to school by bus?	Do you like maths?	Do you do your homework in the afternoon?
Do you do your homework in the evening?	Do you like pets?	Do you collect stamps?	Do you sometimes go to pop concerts?
Do you sometimes go to discos?	Do your friends often ride their bikes?	Do you like going shopping?	Do you buy sweets with your pocket money?
Do you get money if you help your parents?	Do you get enough pocket money?	Do you sometimes get money as a present?	Do you buy clothes with your pocket money?
Do you have any brothers or sisters?	Do you live in a house?	Do you live in town?	

21. Parts of the Body

Words

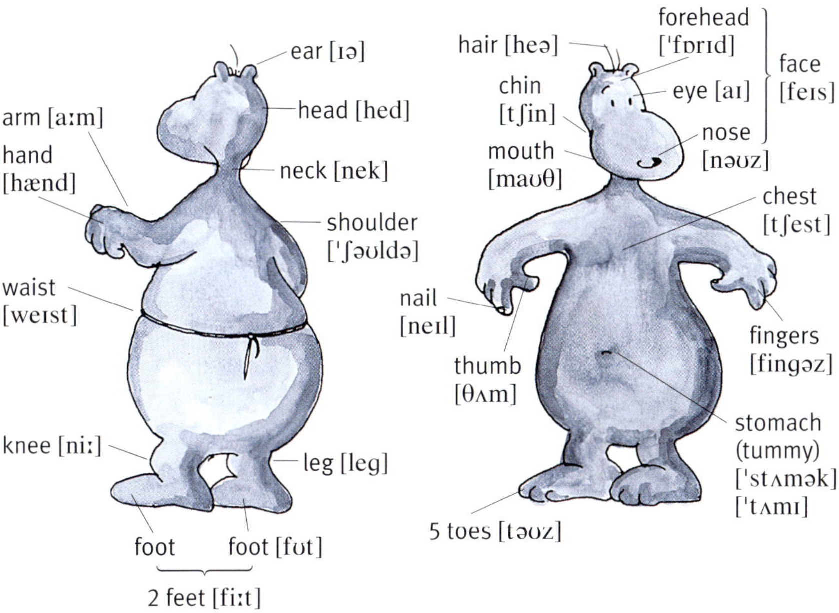

21.1 What is it?

Fill in the gaps.

1.  It's on your neck. It's your ....

2.  You can smell with it. It's your ....

3.  You can speak with it. It's your ....

4.  You can hear with them. They're your ....

5.  Its colour can be brown, grey, black, red or fair. It's your ....

6.  You have five .... on each ....

7.  You have one .... on each ....

8.  You can see with them. They're your ....

21.2 Mixed exercise

Put the right word into the gap.

1. The little boy rides on his father's shoulders. (shoulders / ~~nose~~)
2. The neck is between the .... and the .... (chest / hands / ears / head)
3. The girl with the long .... runs very fast. (toes / legs)
4. Little Brenda has eaten too much cake, now her .... hurts. (leg / tummy)

neighbour – Nachbar

5. Our neighbour wears a hat on his .... (ears / head)
6. The old gentleman has grey .... (knees / hair)
7. The teacher says, "Put your .... up." (hand / face)
8. It's wintertime and cold. Sarah runs home. She has a red .... (tummy / nose)
9. Karen has very good .... She hears very well. (feet / ears)
10. Wash your .... before you eat. (hair / hands)
11. Tom has good .... He can see the little bird. (toes / eyes)
12. Jessica plays the guitar with her .... (fingers / feet)

21.3 What can you do with what?

Choose the right words from the list.

with your mouth you can
- call
- . at
- d . . . k
- . . ea .
- . . . gh
- sm . . .
- ki . .
- ta . k

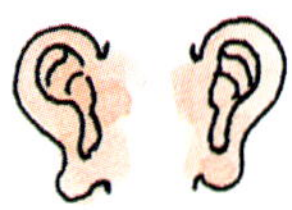

with your ears you can hear and listen to your
- s . . n . s
- w . . . s
- m . . . c
- te . . . . r

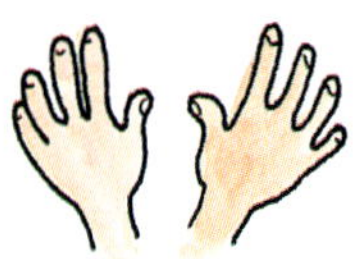

with your hands you can
- w . . . .
- . arr .
- l . . t
- . oi . .
- d . . w

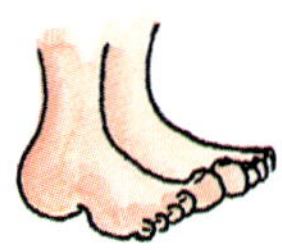

with your legs and feet you can
- w . . k
- d . . . e
- . u . .
- . um .
- . t . . d
- r . n
- h . . . y

eat – carry – dance – music – point – walk – laugh – draw – kiss – speak – rush – words – write – drink – teacher – sounds – run – smile – hurry – jump – call – lift – stand – talk

21.4 An alien

Arrange the letters of the words below in the right order and fill in.

1. cenk 2. hdna 3. ofot 4. nich 5. eekn 6. are 7. grefin 8. eto
9. eons 10. toumh 11. adeh 12. egl 13. roleduhs 14. tsech
15. machost 16. raih 17. bumth 18. yee 19. daeehorf

21.5 Monsters

Match the monsters with their descriptions. Fill in the matching numbers.

1

2

3

This monster is very big. It's got a round head with five eyes, two noses and one mouth. It's got three arms, six hands with three fingers each, four legs and four big feet. ◯

This monster has got three eyes, three noses and two mouths. It's got two arms and two hands with four fingers each. It's got six legs. ◯

This monster is big and fat. It's got four arms, very big hands, three very long legs and small knees. It's got four big eyes and six ears. It's got a big mouth with sharp teeth. ◯

Words

How to describe a person

moustache [mə'sta:ʃ] – Schnurrbart
square – quadratisch

face		eyes (colour)	eyes (type)
 round		blue	 large
 square		brown	 small
		black	
		green	
		hazel	

fringe – Pony

hair (colour)	hair (type)	
red	 curly/wavy	 fringe
brown	 straight	 pony-tail
blond	 bald (no hair)	
black		
grey		
fair/dark		

nose	mouth	ears
 large/big	 small	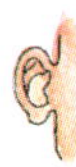 large
 small	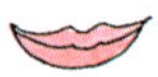 wide	 small
 straight	 full lips	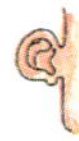 round
	 thin/narrow lips	 close to head

height – Größe
build – Körperbau
solid – untersetzt

height			build		
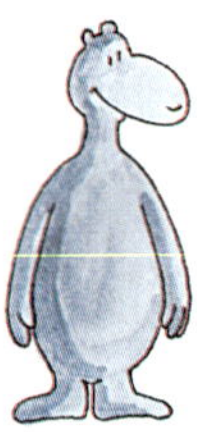			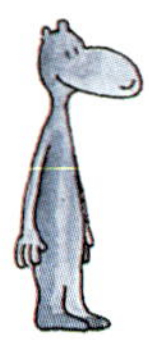		
tall	medium size	short	thin	big/solid	plump/fat

21.6 Funny faces

Here are three faces. Which one is Jack? Which one is Bill? Which one is Ned? Write the names under their pictures.

....

....

....

Bill has got long curly hair. His nose is small and short. His eyes are small, his mouth is narrow. He's got quite a long beard and a moustache.

Ned has got long straight hair. His nose is big and his mouth wide. His eyes are round and large.

Jack's got a square face. His nose is small and his mouth is narrow. He's nearly bald and wears glas-ses.

21.7 Play this game with a friend

Dialogue

Here are some more faces. Tell your friend about them. Don't say the person's name. See if your friend can guess which person you are thinking of.

Nick

Coco

Jojo

Edward

Aunt Mary

Elisabeth

22. Clothes

Words

A fashion show

! Weil eine Hose zwei Hosenbeine hat, gibt es das englische Wort ***trousers*** nur im Plural: *Your trousers are too tight*. Das gilt ebenso für ***jeans/shorts***. Eine Hose heißt: ***a pair of trousers***.

Reading

22.1 A puzzle game

Shorts and trousers

Tom, Dick and Jack are wearing shirts and trousers. Their shirts are red or blue. Their trousers are green or blue. Two boys are wearing green trousers. One boy is wearing a red shirt and green trousers. One boy is wearing a blue shirt and green trousers. One boy is wearing a red shirt and blue trousers. Jack and Tom are wearing red shirts. Dick is wearing green trousers.

What colour of shirt and trousers is Dick wearing?

22.2 What are they wearing?

Write the names of the clothes into the labels.

22.3 A clothes puzzle

Write the names of the clothes on the lines.

Clothes

1. tcao ___coat___
2. sneja ___jeans___
3. otobs ________
4. rusotrse ________
5. eit ________
6. koscs ________
7. lasdnas ________
8. retaews ________
9. gracdnia ________
10. ebluos ________
11. sehos ________
12. cjtkae ________

22.4 The clothes monster

Write the names in the grid.

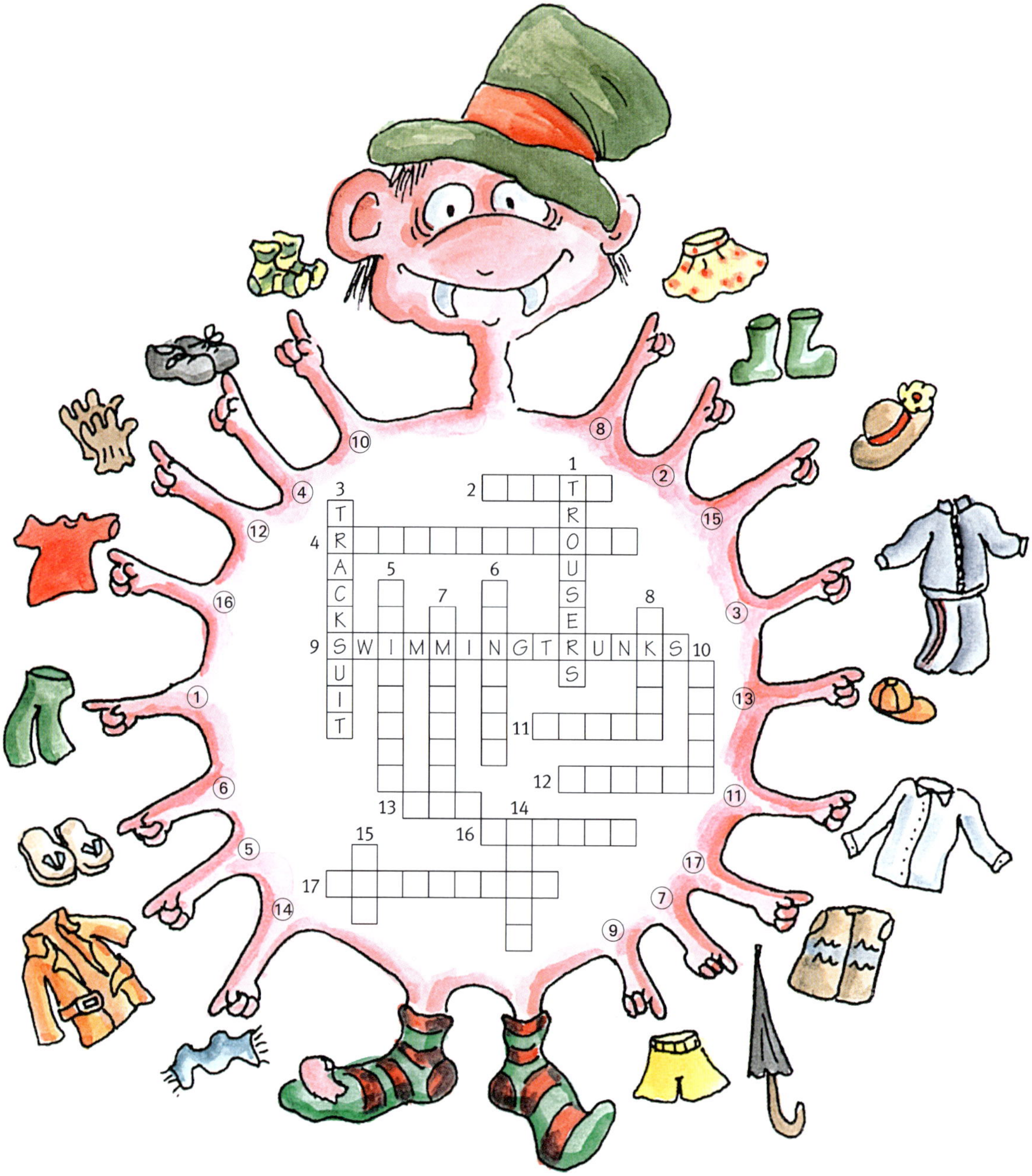

Words

Describing clothes

Material

Woll ... | Seiden ... | Baumwoll ... | Leder

Looks

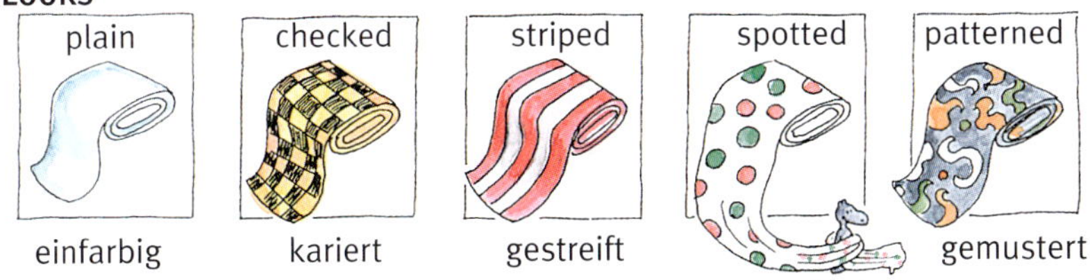

einfarbig | kariert | gestreift | gepunktet | gemustert

gut sitzend | kurz | weit | lang | eng

langärmlig | kurzärmlig | ohne Ärmel | übergroß

22.5 What can you see?

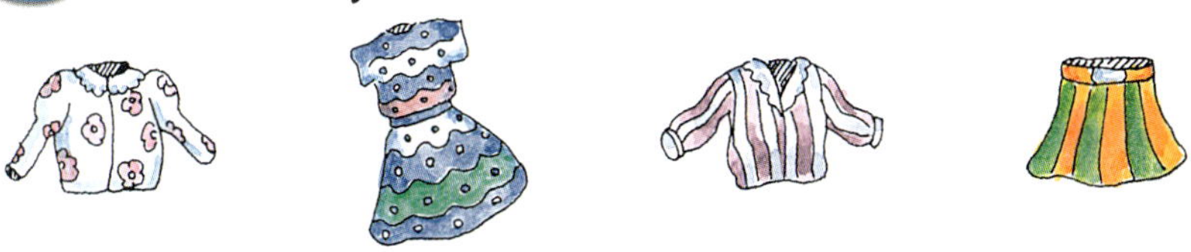

a flowered blouse ....

....

22.6 Clothes and colours

Read the text and colour the clothes.

Colour the striped suit blue, the plain skirt red, the sandals brown, the coat green, the spotted tie blue, the pair of jeans blue, the anorak grey, the gloves brown, the checked shirt pink, the shorts red, the striped scarf red and yellow, the socks brown, the cap red and white, the flowered blouse blue, the leather belt black, the cardigan yellow, the sleeveless jumper orange, the shoes black, the T-shirt white, the boots yellow, the jacket brown, the flowered dress blue and yellow, the spotted skirt light yellow, the leather jacket black, the watch blue.

22.7 Describe Penny the punk

Write in your exercise book.

Hello! I'm Harold Brown. I'm with my sister Penelope, called Penny the punk. I'm wearing a yellow pullover, a black leather belt, a pair of striped trousers, grey spotted socks – (you can't see them) – and yellow and blue trainers. Penny is wearing a striped T-shirt, ...

Example:

Penny is wearing a striped T-shirt, ...

23. Houses and Homes

Words

detached house

semi-detached houses

terraced houses

bungalow

flat – Wohnung

church

factory

skyscraper

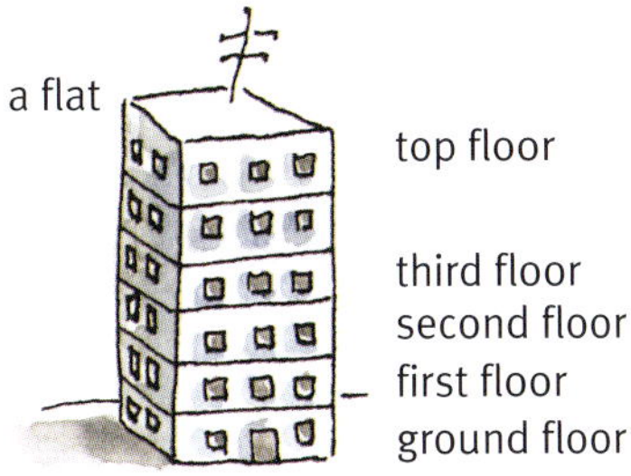

block of flats

kennel

castle

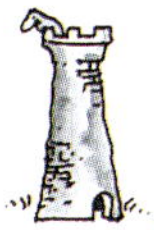
tower

farmhouse

cottage

treehouse

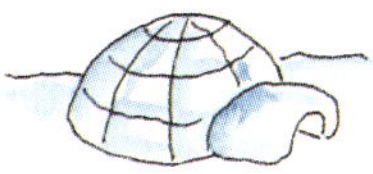
igloo

lighthouse

palace

23.1 There are many kinds of homes

Fill in.

You may live in a  .... in a town

or in a  .... in a big city

or in a  .... in the country.

You can also live in a  ....

Another kind of house is a  .... where

you may find a  ....

Here is an  .... His home is

an  ....

I have a  ...., his home is

a  ....

23.2 Over to you: Where I live

Describe your home. Make notes.

1. Do you live in a house or a flat? Yes, I do / No, I don't.
2. If it is a house, what kind of house is it? It's a ....

town-house – farmhouse – detached – semi-detached – terraced

3. If it is a flat, what is the building like? Which floor is your flat on? ....

....

a block of flats on the ground floor – on the ... floor

4. Have you got a garden? What is it like? ....

....

a large garden at the back of the house – no garden – a small garden –
a garden where children can play

5. Does your house / flat have a balcony? What do you use it for? ....

....

hanging out the washing – growing pot plants – having meals in summer

Write sentences. Use your notes and write in your exercise book.

Today I want to tell you about ... where I live. ... is

not far from ... . It is ... . There are ... . Our ... has got ... .

Reading

23.3 Peter's house

Have a look at the drawing. Read the text and follow the description.

I live in a semi-detached house. I am very happy in our house, because I have a room of my own.

Our house has got two floors, a ground floor and a first floor. My room is on the first floor. From my window I can look into the street. I like to look out of the window and watch people passing our house.

pass – vorbeigehen

When you enter our house by the front door, you come into the hall. There are some pegs to hang the coats on. Stairs lead to the first floor.

On the ground floor is the living room, the bathroom, a kitchen and my parents' bedroom. The most important room on the ground floor is the living room, because the TV and my parents' stereo are in there. When my parents are out I like to sit on the comfortable sofa and listen to CDs or watch television.

important – wichtig

comfortable – bequem

The kitchen is small, but there's enough room for a table and four chairs, the electric stove, a dishwasher, the fridge and two cupboards.

On weekdays we have our meals in the kitchen, but on Sundays we eat in the living room.

In my parents' bedroom there is a big double bed, a dressing table with a mirror for my mother and a wardrobe for clothes. Sometimes I like to go into this room and lie down a little in the big double bed.

Upstairs there is my bedroom and my sister's bedroom. We have a small toilet.

Then there are stairs that lead up to the attic. It is full of cupboards and wardrobes and chests and boxes. In winter I can play table tennis or darts there. In summer it is mostly too warm under the roof.

tool – Werkzeug

We've got a cellar, too. We keep our garden things there, our bikes and our tools. A washing machine is down there, too. I sometimes help to carry the washing upstairs and to hang it on the line in our small back garden.

Answer the questions.

1. What kind of house does Peter live in? He lives in a ....
2. How many rooms are there altogether? ....
3. Why is Peter happy in his house? ....
4. What is the first room you get to after having entered the house? ....
5. Why is the living room very important for Peter? ....
6. Where do they have meals on weekdays? ....
7. What can Peter see from the window of his room? ....
8. Is there a room under the roof? If so, what is it called? ....
9. Where is the washing machine? ....
10. Is there a garden? ....

24. The *there*-Structure / Die *there*-Struktur

There is	no mirror in the kitchen.	Es gibt keinen Spiegel in der Küche.
	a TV set in the study.	Es gibt einen Fernseher im Arbeitszimmer.
	a sofa in the sitting room.	Es ist ein Sofa im Wohnzimmer.
There are	two beds in the bedroom.	Es gibt zwei Betten im Schlafzimmer.
	no posters in the bathroom.	Es sind keine Poster im Badezimmer.
	books on the shelf.	Es befinden sich Bücher im Regal.

Mit ***there is*** / ***there's*** oder ***there are*** kannst du Sätze beginnen, um auf das Vorhandensein von Dingen oder Personen hinzuweisen. Im Deutschen: es gibt, es ist, es sind, es befindet sich. ***There is*** (*short form* ***there's***) wird verwendet, wenn es sich um eine Person oder einen Gegenstand handelt. Bei mehreren Personen oder Dingen steht ***there are***.

Grammar

Question form

In der Frageform stellst du wieder um.

Predicate	Subject	
Is there	only one window in this room?	Yes, there is.
Are there	two doors in this room?	No, there aren't.
Is there	a new teacher in our school?	Yes, there is.
Are there	two new girls in our class?	No, there aren't.

In der Frageform wird – wie im Deutschen – Subjekt und Prädikat einfach vertauscht.

Grammar

24.1 What a funny house!

Schau dir das Bild an! Was stimmt nicht mit dem Haus?

Look at the picture and say what is wrong with the house.

1. There is .... a toilet upstairs in the sitting room.
2. There are .... stairs upstairs in the study.
3. There .... a bathtub downstairs in the children's bedroom.
4. .... pigs downstairs in the ....
5. .... a coffee pot hanging from the ceiling.
6. .... clothes hanging on a line in the bedroom.

bathtub – Badewanne
pig – Schwein
ceiling – Decke

Now ask questions about the funny house and give the answers.

bookshelf – Bücherregal

7. Is there .... a bookshelf upstairs in the bathroom? Yes, there is ....
8. .... a shower upstairs in the sitting room? Yes, ...
9. .... pigs downstairs in the bedroom? No, there aren't.
10. .... books on the shelf? Yes, ...
11. .... a washing machine on the bed? Yes, ...
12. .... a TV set downstairs in the kitchen? No, ...
13. .... a boy sitting downstairs on the chair? No, ...

24.2 Stranger in a town

You want to know where some places are.

Du bist fremd in einer Stadt und willst wissen, wo die Orte sich befinden.
Ordne zuerst die Namen den Bildern zu.
Formuliere dann Fragen und Antworten.
– no
+ yes

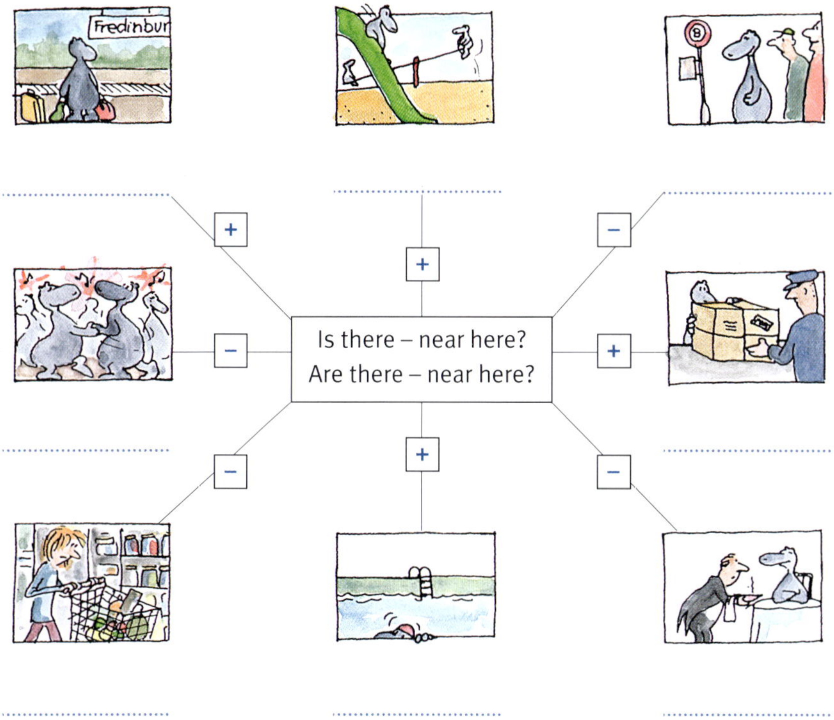

supermarket – post office – swimming pool – station – playground –
bus stop – restaurant – discos

playground – Spielplatz

Example:

+ A: Excuse me, is there a swimming-pool near here?
  B: Yes, there is a very nice swimming pool over there.

– A: Excuse me, are there any discos near here?
  B: No, there are no discos near here.

+ A: Excuse me, ...?
  B: Yes, ...

– A: Excuse me, ...?
  B: No, ...

Continue in your exercise book.

25. Prepositions / Präpositionen

Die verschiedenen Präpositionen

Präpositionen (Verhältniswörter) geben das Verhältnis von Personen, Dingen oder Sachverhalten zueinander an. Es gibt

1. ***Prepositions of place:***	Sie drücken aus, an welchem Ort sich jemand/etwas befindet (auf die Frage **wo**?).
2. ***Prepositions of movement:***	Sie drücken aus, in welche Richtung sich jemand/etwas bewegt (auf die Frage **wohin**? oder **woher**?).
3. ***Prepositions of time:***	Sie drücken aus, zu welcher Zeit oder in welchem Zeitraum sich etwas ereignet (auf die Frage **wann**?).

Grammar

Prepositions of place – Ortsangaben

Where?

at – an

on – auf

under – unter

by/near – nahe

behind – hinter

beside – neben

between – zwischen

in front of – vor, gegenüber

on the left – links

on the right – rechts

in/inside – in

opposite – gegenüber

over – über

above – oberhalb

below – unterhalb

next to – neben

round – um

among – unter

in the middle of – in der Mitte von

25.1 In front of / behind / on / under / between

The children are playing hide and seek. Where are they?

1. Brenda is standing in front of the garage door. She is looking for her friends. 2. Brian is sitting .... the table. 3. Anne is hiding .... the tree. 4. Tony is lying .... the roof of the garage. 5. Jenny is hiding .... the house. 6. The dog is sitting .... the chair.

25.2 A circus parade

Fill in the prepositions.

1. The monkey is walking behind the giraffe.
2. The elephant is walking .... of the zebra.
3. The zebra is walking .... the elephant and the giraffe.
4. The lion is walking .... the clown.
5. The clown is walking .... the horse.
6. The bear is at the end.
7. The camel is walking .... the monkey and the horse.
8. The lion is walking .... of the bear.
9. The giraffe is walking .... the monkey and the zebra.
10. The horse is walking .... the camel.

25.3 The thief

Number the sentences in the correct order. Then write them in your exercise book.

- ☐ Peggy is standing near the sitting room table now and looking for the recorder.
- ☐ She is lying on the sofa and crying.
- [1] Peggy is sitting at her desk doing her homework.
- ☐ She is standing opposite the hall door and telephoning the police.
- ☐ Now he is in the sitting room. He is taking the recorder.
- ☐ A man is standing at the window. He is looking at the cassette recorder.

25.4 Where are they?

Fill in the correct prepositions.

The girl is sitting ……on…… the chair.
(behind, on, by, under)

The boy is standing ………………… the trees.
(beside, next to, between, in front of)

Tony is hiding ………………… the door.
(before, at, behind, in front of)

The oranges are ………………… the box.
(into, in, on, out of)

The car is waiting ………………… the house.
(beside, in the middle of, in, in front of)

The dog is lying ………………… the car.
(above, under, near, at)

Prepositions of movement – Richtungsangaben

Grammar

Where to? Where from?

up – hinauf

down – hinunter

across – quer durch

over – über

round – um

along – entlang

after – hinter

towards – auf ... zu

from – von

through – durch

to – zu

against – gegen

out of – aus (... heraus)

into – in (... hinein)

about – hin und her

past – an ... vorbei

on to – auf (... hinauf)

25.5 What are the people doing?

Fill in the prepositions.

The pupils are running ....to.... school.
(out of, into, to)

The man is going .... the street.
(across, over, round, along)

Molly is running .... the stairs.
(over, down, up, above)

The dog is running .... the girls.
(against, into, through, after)

The boy is jumping .... the gate.
(about, on to, over, round)

The man is running .... the wall.
(out of, against, through, across)

Mr. Brown is going .... the house.
(from, past, on to, into)

25.6 The fly

Write down what the fly is doing.

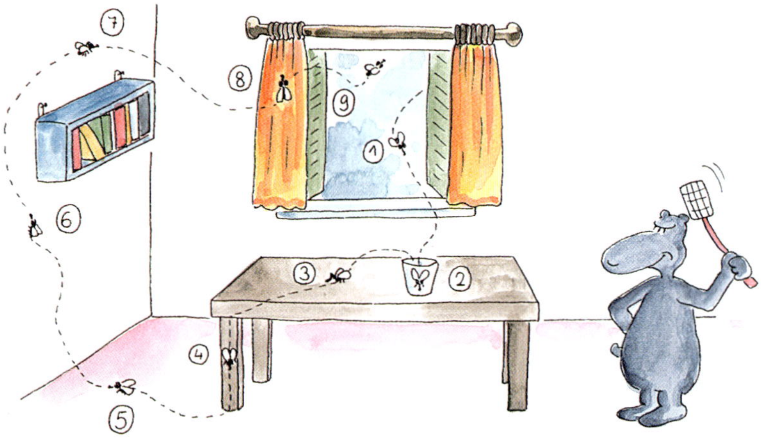

1. It is coming through .... the window. (come)
2. It .... the glass. (fly)
3. It .... the table. (sit)
4. Now it .... the table leg. (go)
5. Now it .... the floor. (walk)
6. It .... the wall. (climb)
7. Now it .... the bookshelf. (fly)
8. It .... the curtain. (climb)
9. At last it .... the window. (fly)

25·7 At the circus

Fill in the prepositions.

Let's talk about the picture! It is a circus. Can you see the big elephant? It is walking .... the circus ring. Try to find the horse which is running .... it. A clown is sitting .... a car. Another clown is falling .... There are three boys in the circus. They are riding bikes. One of them rides ...., one behind and one is .... them. Can you see the clown with the dog? The dog is running .... the clown. Can you see the two men flying .... the air? Two others are going .... and .... Two girls are standing .... their horses. They are riding .... a man. One clown is not in the circus ring. He is sitting with his back .... the wall.

Lösungen

1. The Indefinite Article / Der unbestimmte Artikel

Seite 7 1.1

2. This is an orange.
3. This is an American.
4. This is an elephant.
5. This is an umbrella.
6. This is a book.
7. This is a uniform.

2. I have got a big orange.
3. I have got an American book.
4. I have got a toy elephant.
5. I have got a small umbrella.
6. I have got an old book.
7. I have got a nice uniform.

Seite 8 1.2

a workbook / an old teddy / a pencil case / a sandwich / an English book / an exercise book / an empty bottle / a new lipstick

Seite 8 1.3

a boy / a mouth / a tree / a car / a train / a house / a helicopter / a girl / a clock
an egg / an ear / an apple / an Englishman / an eye / an orange / an idea

2. School Things

Seite 9 2.1

(von links nach rechts)
a textbook, a pen, an atlas, sheets of paper, felt-tip pens, a satchel, a ruler, pencils, a schoolbag, a picture, a pencil case, a calculator, a biro, paperclips, a rubber (eraser), coloured pencils, glue, a folder, scissors, a dictionary, chalk and duster, a globe

Seite 10 2.2

1. textbook	4. pen	7. rubber
2. ruler	5. biro	8. pencil sharpener
3. pencil	6. satchel	9. pencil case

Seite 10 2.3

1. pencil	4. pencil case	7. workbook
2. ruler	5. exercise book	8. biro
3. calculator	6. folder	9. sandwich

Seite 10 2.4

Der Lösungssatz lautet:
In my bag is a green pencil case, a ruler, a white rubber, a textbook, a red felt-tip pen, a blue pencil, a sharpener, a pad, a yellow pen and an exercise book.

Seite 11 2.5

Die "school things" in der "mindmap" lauten: schoolbag, textbook, ruler, scissors, glue, calculator, folder, pencil case, pen, biro, pencils, rubber (eraser)

Seite 11 2.6

Schreibe einfach auf, was du in deiner Schultasche findest. Gib auch die Anzahl an.
Zum Beispiel:
In my schoolbag I have got 6 books – an English book, a German textbook, a geography book, a maths book, a songbook and a biology book. Then I have got a pen, 2 felt-tip pens and 6 biros. I have also got 7 exercise books and one pencil case in my schoolbag.
In my schoolbag there is a ruler, a rubber (eraser) and a little teddy bear. It helps me to get good marks at school.

2.7 *Seite 12*

Early in the morning Billy gets up and goes to his desk. He puts a maths book, an English book and a geography book into his schoolbag. Then he takes his schoolbag and runs out of the house to go to school. His mother is standing at the door and tells him that there is no school today because it is Sunday.

3 . In the Classroom

3.1 *Seite 13*

1. classroom
2. pupil
3. pen / pencil / biro
4. board / blackboard
5. cupboard
6. chair
7. map
8. schoolbag / satchel
9. chalk
10. ruler

3.2 *Seite 14*

Ich habe mich verspätet.	I'm sorry, I'm late.
Wie spricht man dieses Wort aus?	How do you pronounce this word?
Wie heißt das auf Englisch?	What's that in English?
Ich finde das prima.	Great! Fine! That's a good idea!
Ich verstehe leider nicht.	I'm sorry, I don't understand.
Ich habe mein ... vergessen.	I have forgotten my ...
Kannst du das bitte noch einmal sagen?	Could you say that again, please?
Was heißt das auf Deutsch?	What's that in German?
Darf ich lesen?	May I read?
Was heißt / bedeutet ...?	What does ... mean?
Welche Hausaufgaben haben wir auf?	What homework have we got?
Es ist langweilig.	Boring!
Darf ich an die Wandtafel schreiben?	May I write on the board?
Das ist nicht wahr.	That's not true.
Ich bin an der Reihe.	It's my turn.
Kann ich bitte dein ... benutzen?	Can I use your ..., please?

3.3 *Seite 15*

One day, Sandy meets a lion and he takes her to school on his back. The teacher stops taking the register, when she sees the little girl and the lion. She looks at the lion and all the other pupils look at the lion, wondering what the teacher is going to say. The teacher says to the little girl, "You know you are not allowed to bring pets to school." The lion begins to swish his tail. The little girl says, "This is my friend, who is coming to school with me." The teacher asks his name. The little girl tells her his name is Noil. The teacher writes the name down in her register and the lion can stay in the classroom with Sandy.

3.4 *Seite 16*

Stelle dir deine Mitschüler vor, dann die Ausstattung des Klassenzimmers. Zum Schluss schreibe etwas über deine besten Freunde. Der Text könnte wie folgt lauten:

In my class there are 18 girls and 8 boys. That makes 26 children. There are 6 German boys and 15 German girls. That makes 21 German children.
There are 2 boys and 3 girls from other countries. That makes 5 children from other countries. In my class are girls and boys from Spain, Poland and Turkey.
In my classroom are 13 tables, 27 chairs, 8 posters, 3 pictures, 2 boards, 4 windows, 1 door, 1 computer, 1 overhead projector and a teacher's desk.
The objects in my schoolbag are 1. exercise books, 2. pencil case, 3. felt-tip pens, 4. textbooks, 5. calculator, 6. ruler, 7. ...
My best friend is Henry. He is ten years old. His address is Steinfurter Allee 3, 80711 Munich. My other friends are Peter, Rolf and Georgina from Poland.

4. Cardinal Numbers / Grundzahlen

Seite 18 **4.1**

1. five	4. eleven	7. nine
2. six	5. six	8. five
3. twelve	6. two	9. three

Seite 18 **4.2**

Number of legs on two dogs = eight
Number of hours in a day = twenty-four
Number of quarters in a half = two
Number of days in a week = seven
Number of balls in a football match = one
Number of legs on a chair = four
Number of months in a year = twelve
Number of all your fingers = ten
Number of toes on one foot = five
Number of zeroes in a million = six
Number of arms on a monkey = two

Seite 19 **4.3**

Die Telefonnummern lauten von links nach rechts:

1. one – o – three – two – three – one
2. double one – double seven – two – o
3. one – four – eight – seven – two – o
4. one – eight – nine – four – eight – o
5. two – one – five – o – double eight

6. two – five – three – eight – six – five
7. three – four – double five – seven – eight
8. three – four – six – double four – five
9. four – two – three – five – one – eight
10. double four – one – double o – five

11. four – seven – two – double five – two
12. five – o – one – double four – seven
13. six – five – o – three – eight – one
14. six – nine – o – nine – three – one
15. seven – two – o – three – o – five

Seite 19 **4.4**

Brenda = five – eight – three – two – one – nine
Nancy = double seven – double eight – double one
Fiona = six – eight – four – six
Janet = three – four – six – eight – one – o
Colin = four – three – double o – four – seven
Brenda is talking to Nancy.
Fiona is talking to Colin.

4.5 *Seite 20*

Denke daran, wie oft du telefonierst, auch mit Handy, und worüber du sprichst. Deine Lösung könnte wie folgt lauten:
I often phone my friends, and we talk for a long time. My mother is sometimes angry when I phone too much and don't do my homework. I mostly phone my best friend Richard. We talk about school, our classmates and our teachers. Sometimes we talk about problems with our homework, but not very often. Twice a week I phone my aunt Mary. She is very nice and I like her very much.

4.7 *Seite 20*

twenty-one = 21	thirty-seven = 37	eight = 8
twenty = 20	sixty-three = 63	eighty-four = 84
seventy = 70	ninety = 90	eighty = 80
a hundred = 100	sixty = 60	fifty = 50
ninety-eight = 98	thirty-two = 32	forty-nine = 49
forty = 40	fifty-seven = 57	seventy-six = 76
fifteen = 15	thirty = 30	

4.8 *Seite 21*

Erfrage die Einzelheiten, die du nicht weißt, und schreibe die Zahlen aus.

5. Ordinal Numbers / Ordnungszahlen

5.1 *Seite 24*

1st – first / 2nd – second / 3rd – third / 4th – fourth / 5th – fifth / 6th – sixth / 7th – seventh / 8th – eighth / 9th – ninth / 10th – tenth / 11th – eleventh / 12th – twelfth

5.2 *Seite 24*

q-u-e-s-t-i-o-n

5.3 *Seite 25*

1st = Mädchen	8th = Eimer	15th = Briefmarke
2nd = Boot	9th = Lampe	16th = Tür
3rd = Apfel	10th = Ball	17th = Fahrrad
4th = Bleistift	11th = Verkehrsampel	18th = Handtasche
5th = Haus	12th = Flasche	19th = Tisch
6th = Teppich	13th = Schuh	20th = Vogel
7th = Auto	14th = Junge	

5.4 *Seite 26*

88th, 20th, 9th, 50th, 4th, 36th, 3rd, 12th, 57th, 18th, 1st, 11th

5.5 *Seite 26*

Deine Lösung könnte wie folgt aussehen:
Today is the fourth day of the month.
This month is the fifth month of the year.
We are now in the sixteenth hour of the day.
I have had my tenth birthday and I am now in my eleventh year.
I am in my fifth year at school. I am the second child in my family.
I am usually the third in my family to leave home in the morning.
I am usually the first in my family to go to bed at night.

6. Days of the Week

Seite 27 **6.1**

(von links nach rechts:)
Friday, Monday, Tuesday
Thursday is missing.

(von oben nach unten:)
Saturday, Sunday, Wednesday

Seite 27 **6.2**

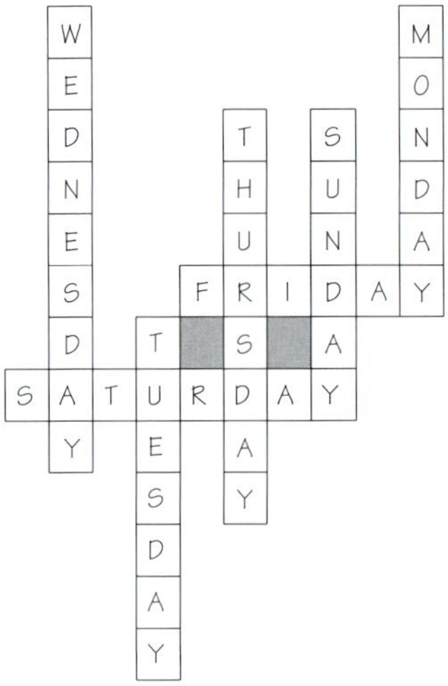

Seite 28 **6.3**

April 2nd = Thursday
April 1st = Wednesday
April 3rd = Friday
April 4th = Saturday

April 5th = Sunday
March 31st = Tuesday
March 30th = Monday

Seite 29 **6.5**

On Tuesdays I go to art school.
On Wednesdays I watch TV and visit my friend.
On Thursdays I help my father.
On Fridays I read a book.
On Saturdays I work in the garden and go to the disco.
On Sundays I sleep late and eat out at a restaurant.

Seite 29 **6.6**

Jimmy sleeps late and he goes to the park with his friends.
Brenda plays with her mum and dad and eats out at a restaurant with them.
Tom goes to church and then visits his grandmother.
Michael is in the garden and has a picnic there.
Sarah has a big breakfast but no dinner.

7. Months of the Year

Seite 30 **7.1**

1. March	5. December	9. November
2. July	6. June	10. September
3. May	7. August	11. April
4. February	8. January	12. October

Seite 31 **7.2**

January / February / March / April / May / June / July / August / September / October / November / December

7.3 *Seite 31*

January is the first month of the year.
February is the second month of the year.
April is the fourth month of the year.
August is the eighth month of the year.
September is the ninth month of the year.
December is the twelfth month of the year.
May is the fifth month of the year.
November is the eleventh month of the year.
March is the third month of the year.

7.4 *Seite 32*

20.2. the twentieth of February / February 20th
1.1. the first of January / January 1st
30.3. the thirtieth of March / March 30th
3.11. the third of November / November 3rd
31.12. the thirty-first of December / December 31st
14.5. the fourteenth of May / May 14th
22.9. the twenty-second of September / September 22nd
9.7. the ninth of July / July 9th
5.4. the fifth of April / April 5th
8.8 the eighth of August / August 8th
2.6. the second of June / June 2nd

7.5 *Seite 33*

Dad's birthday is on the seventeenth of July.
Fred's birthday is on the first of April.
Aunt Mary's birthday is on the eighteenth of October.
Pam's birthday is on the twenty-sixth of January

7.6 *Seite 33*

Deine Lösung könnte ungefähr wie folgt lauten:
My birthday is on the eleventh of October. My mother's birthday is on the third of February. My father's birthday is on the first of January. I was born in 19..., my father was born in 19..., my mother in 19...

7.7 *Seite 34*

It's time to make my birthday wish.
What day's today? It's my birthday!
It's fun to bake a birthday cake.

7.8 *Seite 34*

Dear Claudia,
Many thanks for your letter. I hope you and your family are well. We are all fine.
I'm writing this letter on Sunday, the twenty-first of January. It's winter here now. It's raining a lot at the moment. I can't cycle this weekend, so I'm staying at home listening to music, watching TV and writing this letter. Next Wednesday is my birthday and Mum is making me a big birthday cake. She's got eleven candles for it. All my friends will come to my birthday party and we'll dance and sing. My birthday also means more pocket money.
Please write soon!
Best wishes
Michael

Seite 35 **7.9**

1. Susan's birthday is on the eleventh of October.
2. Susan is eleven years old.
3. In the morning Susan opens her birthday cards.
4. She gets seventeen cards from her family and friends.
5. She gets a new bike from her parents and a horse book from her brother. Her aunt gives her £ 25.
6. Susan's friends play a lot of games, dance and eat birthday cake.

Seite 35 **7.10**

Überlege, was du an deinem Geburtstag so alles tust. Bilde dann Sätze aus der "mindmap". Dein Text könnte wie folgt lauten:
On my birthday I invite my friends. We play games, dance or listen to music. Sometimes I go to the cinema with my friends.

8. The Time

Seite 36 **8.1**

1. wristwatch
2. grandfather clock
3. alarm clock
4. pocket watch

Seite 38 **8.2**

2. ten past ten
3. half past six
4. quarter past five
5. twelve o'clock
6. quarter past ten
7. four o'clock
8. half past three
9. quarter to seven
10. twenty-five to four
11. five to twelve
12. twenty to eight
13. twenty to nine
14. two o'clock
15. quarter to nine
16. ten to seven

Seite 39 **8.3**

It's twenty to four · It's ten to two · It's five to seven · It's twenty-five to ten · It's twenty to eight

It's five past seven · It's twenty-five past one · It's ten past eleven · It's twenty past three · It's twenty-five past nine

Seite 40 **8.4**

Saturday morning at the Carters'
Mrs. Carter gets up at (a) quarter past seven.
Mr. Carter gets up at half past seven.
At eight o'clock Mr. and Mrs. Carter have breakfast.
After breakfast Mr. Carter reads the newspaper.
Mrs. Carter calls the children.
Susan gets up at once, but Tom is a sleepyhead.
He lies in bed until nine o'clock.
At (a) quarter to nine Mrs. Carter goes into the kitchen and makes breakfast for the children.

At half past nine Susan and Tom take the breakfast things to the kitchen.
Mr. Carter does the washing-up, and Susan helps her father.
At ten past ten they go shopping.
Susan and Tom play with their friends.
At ten to one they all sit down to lunch in the dining room.

9. Countries, Peoples and Languages

9.1 *Seite 42*

Cindy is in Russia. Bill is in Greece. Patty is in Great Britain. Rick is in Germany. Susan is in the USA. Ramesh is in France. Sally is in Italy.

9.3 *Seite 43*

Halte dich an den Beispielsatz und bilde ähnliche Sätze über die anderen Nationalitäten.
2. Björn is from Denmark. He is Danish. He speaks Danish etc.

9.4 *Seite 44*

Vergleiche das Muster auf S. 44.
Du musst nur die Begriffe aus der ersten Spalte durch die Angaben aus den weiteren Spalten ersetzen. Hier noch ein Beispiel (Spalte 2):

What's your name?	↔	My name is Maria.
Where are you from?	↔	I'm from Spain.
Where in Spain?	↔	From Madrid.
What languages do you speak?	↔	Spanish and German.
How many brothers and sisters have you got?	↔	I've got 4 brothers and 2 sisters.
How old are you?	↔	I'm twelve.

9.5 *Seite 44*

Halte dich auch hier an das vorgegebene Muster. Wir geben dir noch zwei weitere Beispiele:
Number 2
Her name is Maria. She comes from Spain. She lives in Madrid. She speaks Spanish and German. She has got four brothers and two sisters. Maria is twelve.
Number 3
His name is Pit. He comes from Holland. He lives in Amsterdam. He speaks Dutch, English and German. Pit has got one sister. He is ten.

9.7 *Seite 46*

1.
    1. Baltic Sea
    2. North Sea
    3. Hanover
    4. Cologne
    5. Nuremberg
    6. Danube
    7. Munich
    8. Rhine

2. The capital of Germany is Berlin.
   Famous places in Germany are for example: the Chiemsee near Munich, the Loreley on the Rhine, the Heidepark near Soltau.
   Longest river: the Elbe
   Highest mountains: The Alps

3. There are about 80 million people in Germany. They speak German and some other languages. The name of the currency is the Euro (€) now.
The most famous person in Germany I think is ...?

4. I live in the south of Germany, in Ingolstadt. My town is between Munich and Nuremberg. It's on the Danube.

10. Singular and Plural / Singular und Plural

Seite 47 **10.1**

There are two boys, nine birds, six balls, two chairs, nine apples, four flags, five pictures, four lamps, two schoolbags, four pears, seven toy cars, eight books, five dolls, three teddy bears, two hats, eleven flowers, one table, one window, one bed.

Seite 49 **10.2**

2. monkey
3. key
4. car
5. dress
6. dish
7. baby
8. pony
9. page
10. boy
11. rose
12. fly
13. spoon
14. bridge
15. horse
16. donkey
17. box
18. house
19. uniform
20. fox
21. glass

Seite 50 **10.4**

I can see four boys, two doors, four trees, five windows, one chimney, two lorries, three boxes, four birds.

Seite 51 **10.5**

fish – women – pence – mice – feet – children – geese – oxen – men – sheep – teeth

Seite 52 **10.6**

men / feet / wolves / sheep / postmen / women / mice / shelves / knives / children / geese / teeth

Seite 52 **10.7**

1. The books are ...
2. The classes end ...
3. The women are ...
4. The children play ...
5. The cats run ...
6. The buses are ...
7. The men are ...
8. The women are ...
9. The mice run ...
10. The boys play ...
11. The thieves steal ...
12. The dishes are ...
13. The shelves are ...
14. The policemen catch ...

11. S-Genitive and Of-Genitive / Der Genitiv

Seite 53 **11.1**

He must clean the children's room.
He must make the family's dinner.
He must wash the neighbour's car.
He must brush Debbie's shoes.
He must repair Tom's bike.

Seite 54 **11.2**

2. It's Ben's satchel.
3. They are the girls' books.
4. They are the children's trousers.
5. It is Peter's doll.
6. It is Susan's table.
7. It is the man's watch.
8. They are the woman's hats.

11.3 Seite 55

the seats of the chairs – the windows of the house – the top of the sideboard – the walls of the sitting room – the carpet of the bedroom

11.4 Seite 55

2. The colour of the house is yellow.
3. The arm of Emily's doll is broken.
4. Father's car is in the garage.
5. The children's room is upstairs.
6. Mother must clean the girls' dresses.
7. The floor of the kitchen is very dirty.
8. The women's clothes are very expensive.

12. Personal Pronouns (subject case) / Personalpronomen

12.1 Seite 57

1. We like speaking English.
2. It is on the desk.
3. She is not at home.
4. He is a good pupil.
5. They are in the cafeteria.
6. She has got one sister and two brothers.
7. It is very cold today.
8. They run into the field.

12.2 Seite 57

Yes it is.
It has got 8 rooms.
Yes, they are.
No, it isn't.
Yes, he can.
No, she can't.
No, they can't.
No, they aren't.

12.3 Seite 58

1. He
2. He
3. They
4. It
5. They
6. She
7. We
8. It
9. They
10. He
11. We
12. He
13. They
14. She
15. He
16. It
17. We
18. They
19. It
20. She
21. She

12.4 Seite 58

1. Fred: I am Fred from Germany.
2. Where are you from? We are from Hamburg.
3. There is Sarah. She is cleaning the bike
4. Where is my book? It isn't here.
5. The children have been playing in the park. They are going home.
6. Look at that car! It is very old.
7. Are you Tom, the new boy?
8. Sharon and Wendy, come here please, you are too noisy.
9. Where are you from? I am from London.
10. Look at those pencils! They are green.

12.5 Seite 59

Robert is my father.
Fred is my grandfather.
Jack is my uncle.
James is my cousin.
Fiona is my aunt.
Brenda is my sister.
Eileen is my grandmother.
Peter is my brother.
Molly is my mother.
Shirley is my cousin.

Seite 59 **12.6**

von links nach rechts:
BROTHER – FATHER – AUNT – GRANDFATHER – FAMILY – COUSIN – SISTER – MOTHER – UNCLE
von oben nach unten:
GRANDMOTHER

Seite 60 **12.7**

A 2 / B 7 / C 8 / D 9 / E 5 / F 4 / G 6 / H 3 / I 1

Seite 60 **12.8**

This is me, Kate.
I'm ten years old. This is Brenda, my little sister. She is 6. This is my father. He is 43 years old and this is my mother. She is 36. They are my parents. This is Peter, my elder brother. He is 15. This is Benny the dog. He is my sister's dog. Here are my father's sister Fiona and her husband Jack. They are my aunt and uncle and they are very nice. Most of all I like my father's mum and dad, my grandparents. They give me extra pocket money. They are really kind.

Seite 61 **12.9**

Robin: Hello, Kate! How are you?
Kate: Fine, thanks.
Robin: Have you got any brothers and sisters?
Kate: Yes, I have.
Robin: How many have you got?
Kate: One brother and one sister.
Robin: I see, how old are they?
Kate: My brother Peter, he is fifteen and my sister Brenda, she is six. Have you got any brothers and sisters?
Robin: Yes, I have. I've got one brother.
Kate: How old is he?
Robin: He is one.

13. Demonstrative Pronouns / Demonstrativpronomen

Seite 63 **13.1**

These are cups. / These are oranges. / This is a spoon. / This is a fork. / These are plates. / This is honey. / Those are plates. / Those are bags. / Those are eggs. / That is a horse show. / That is an apple tree. / Those are lemons.

Seite 63 **13.2**

Are these your trousers? No, they are Peter's.
Is this your pencil? No, it's Karen's.
Is that your hat? No, it's Mum's.
Is that your car? No, it's Mr. Peabody's.
Is that your pullover? No, it's Kim's.
Is this Fred? Yes, it is.
Are those your pictures? No, they are Susan's.
Are those your presents? Yes, they are.
Are those your toys? No, they are Brenda's.

14. The Verb *to be* (Present Tense) / Das Verb „sein" im Präsens

14.1 *Seite 64*

I am a boy.
My name is Peter.
You are a boy / a girl.
Your name is ...
She is my sister.
He is my brother.
It is a book.
We are the Case family.
You are my brother and sister.
They are my family.

14.2 *Seite 65*

1. Henry is a student.
2. He is a good teacher.
3. We are busy.
4. You and Sarah are sisters.
5. The door is closed.
6. I am tired now.
7. This is a good exercise.
8. Mr. and Mrs. Ashing are English.
9. We are brothers.
10. I am happy.
11. You are a good student.
12. She is a good friend.
13. Karen and I are good friends.

14.3 *Seite 66*

It is Saturday afternoon. Mr. and Mrs. Case are in the garden. They are having tea. Kate and Brenda are there, too. Some time later Peter and Shirley are coming. Now the children are playing hide and seek. Kate is counting to ten. Peter is behind a tree. Brenda and Shirley are in the house. Kate says, "Peter, I can't see you. Are you on a tree?" Peter says, "No, I'm not. I am behind the tree." "Brenda and Shirley, where are you? I can't find you," Kate asks. Brenda and Shirley answer, "We are here in the house."

14.4 *Seite 66*

I am on holiday in Soller in Majorca. Today the weather is fine, the wind is nice and cool. Swimming and surfing, enjoying the sun, I can tell you, this is fun. I am glad that there is no school and I am happy that we are here but my friends are so far away and I really miss you!

14.5 *Seite 67*

1. Is she Kate's mother? No, she isn't. She is the English teacher.
2. Am I silly? No, you aren't. You are clever.
3. Is his name Mike? No, it isn't. It is Peter.
4. Is Brenda nine? No, she isn't. She is ten.
5. Are you Colin? No, I am not. I am Joe.
6. Are you her friend? No, I am not. I am her brother.
7. Is that Sue? No, it isn't. It is Peggy.
8. Are you from Denmark? No, I am not. I am from Germany.
9. Is Kate Peter's sister? No, she isn't. She is Lee's sister.

14.6 *Seite 68*

2. am
3. are / are
4. is
5. are / are
6. is
7. are / am
8. Are / am / am
9. Are / aren't / are
10. Am / aren't / are

Seite 68 **14.7**

What is your name? My name is ...
What is your telephone number? My number is ...
Are you a boy or a girl? I am a girl / a boy.
What colour are your eyes? My eyes are ...
What is the name of your school? The name of my school is ...
What is your address? My address is ...
How old are you? I'm ... .
What nationality are you? I am ...
What colour is your hair? My hair is ...
What class are you in? I'm in class ...

Seite 69 **14.8**

1. I am a student.
Henry is a students, too.
This is a good book.
Henry and Maria are good students.
We are good students, too.
Mr. Smith is a teacher.
He is a good teacher.
You are a good student.
Helen and Maria are good students.
They are sisters.
I am very busy today.
Henry is busy today, too.

2. We aren't brothers.
Today isn't Monday.
I am not a good student.
John and I aren't in the same class.
This isn't a good exercice.
The door isn't closed.
We aren't friends.
You and George aren't good friends.
I'm not German.

3. Are they brothers?
Is Miss Jones a good teacher?
Am I happy today?
Are we going to school now?
Are Mr. and Mrs. Ashing English?
Is your father 42?
Are your sisters 12 and 16?
Is this Sarah?

15. The Verb *to have got* / Das Verb „haben“

Seite 70 **15.1**

Has Joe got a pencil case? Yes, he has.
Have Susan and Peter got an English book? Yes, they have.
Have Betty and Paul got a biro? No, they haven't. They've got a pencil.
Has Simon got a ruler? No, he hasn't. He's got a rubber.

Seite 71 **15.2**

Susan has got a doll but she hasn't got brothers and sisters.
Peter has got a lot of books but he hasn't got a guitar.
Fred has got an alarm clock but he hasn't got a watch.
The dog has got a bone but he hasn't got a sausage.
My father and mother have got a car but they haven't got a plane.
Dolly and Molly have got a room but they haven't got a house.

Seite 72 **15.3**

1. Yes, she has.
2. No, she hasn't.
3. Yes, she has.
4. No, he hasn't.
5. No, she hasn't.
6. No, he hasn't.
7. Yes, she has.
8. Yes, she has.

Seite 73 **15.4**

3 chairs — Have you got three chairs?
No, we haven't. We have got two.

4 hats	Have you got four hats? No, we haven't. We have got two.
6 posters	Have you got six posters? No, we haven't. We have got five.
10 apples	Have you got ten apples? No, we haven't. We have got seven.
3 lamps	Have you got three lamps? Yes, we have.
2 tables	Have you got two tables? No, we haven't. We have got one.
2 teddy bears	Have you got two teddy bears? No, we haven't. We have got three.
4 flags	Have you got four flags? Yes, we have.
5 dolls	Have you got five dolls? Yes, we have.
6 books	Have you got six books? Yes, we have.

15.5 Seite 74

Schreibe erst einmal alle Wörter auf, die dir zu den Begriffen in der „mindmap" einfallen.
Fasse dann alles zusammen. Deine Lösung könnte wie folgt lauten:

Family: I've got two aunts and one uncle. I have got a mother and a father and one brother, but no sister. I have also got a grandmother and two cousins.
Room: In my room I have got a bed, a cupboard, a table and two chairs. I have got a TV-set and a radio. I have got lots of books and cassettes, and I have got posters on the wall. I have got a computer, too.
Desk: I have got a ruler, a pencil case, a box of felt-tip pens and lots of biros on my desk. I have also got paperclips and a folder on my desk. Inside my desk I have got some exercise books, a dictionary and some papers.
School: My school has got twenty classrooms. It has got four hundred pupils and twenty-eight teachers. It has got many more rooms for teachers and special subjects. It has got a big schoolyard and some sportsfields.
Schoolbag: In my schoolbag I have got six books, a pencil case, a ruler, a rubber, a calculator and a little globe.

16. Pets

16.1 Seite 75

Susan has got a dog. / Aunt Lily has got a goldfish. / Brenda has got a cat. / Jack has got a rabbit. / Pete has got a guinea pig. / Joe has got a tortoise.

16.2 Seite 76

tail / wings / whiskers / beak / fur / legs

16.3 Seite 77

1. Kevin has got a budgie.
2. The cat sleeps in a basket in Jill's bedroom.
3. A goldfish eats fish food.
4. A cat drinks milk.
5. Sally feeds her hamster before she goes to bed.
6. Peter feeds his dog before he does his homework.

Ersetze die Wörter in dem Mustertext durch die Begriffe, die zu den anderen Kindern gehören.

Seite 78 **16.4**

If you want a hamster, don't forget it is active at night and it sometimes bites.
If you want to forget your pet in winter, get a tortoise.
If you want to keep a cat, don't forget it sometimes brings you dead mice and birds.
If you want to keep a goldfish, don't put the fish tank in direct sunlight.
If you want to keep a mouse, don't forget it smells a bit.
If you want to keep a dog, you must take it for a long walk every day.
If you want to keep a rabbit, you must clean its hutch out twice a week and brush it with a small brush.

Seite 79 **16.6**

Have you got a pet?
What does your pet look like?
What's his name?
How old is he?
Does he need a lot of exercise?
Do you clean his basket often?
Who looks after your dog when you have a lot of homework?

Seite 79 **16.7**

So könnte dein Text aussehen:
There are twenty-two pets in the pet shop. There are three goldfish in a tank. Five mice are in a cage. Two dogs are in a box, one is on the table. There are four cats on the floor. A parrot is hanging from the ceiling (Decke). A canary is sitting in a cage. Three hamsters are in a cage and two guinea pigs.

Seite 80 **16.8**

Denke an dein Haustier oder ein Tier, das du gerne haben möchtest. Schreibe auch über ein Haustier deines Freundes. Deine Lösung könnte wie folgt lauten:

My pet is a cat. Her name is Pussy. – Here is a picture of Pussy. – She eats fish and meat and drinks milk. She likes sitting on my bed but she sleeps in a basket. Sometimes she catches mice and puts them in front of my bed.

My dream pet is a dog. His name is Snap. He eats bones and meat and drinks water. Snap barks loudly when I come home from school and he likes to run about in our garden. He hasn't got a kennel but sleeps in our kitchen.

My friend hat got a pet, too. She has got a hamster. His name is Moppy. He is brown and his feet are white. His tail is short and white. He is very clever and funny. He has got a cage. It is in my friend's room.

17. The Present Progressive Form / Die Verlaufsform der Gegenwart

Seite 81 **17.1**

1. The budgie is singing in the cage.
2. The tortoise is looking at the bird.
3. The fish is dreaming in the tank.
4. The dog is waiting for his food.
5. The cat is sleeping in the basket.
6. The mouse is making fun of the cat.

Seite 82 **17.2**

1. is cooking	5. is watching	9. is cleaning
2. is playing	6. is reading	10. is picking
3. is jumping	7. is riding	
4. is doing	8. is looking	

17.3 *Seite 82*

1. Daddy, what are you doing? I am cooking our meal.
2. Thomas, what are you doing? I am playing football.
3. Cat, what are you doing? I am jumping on the table.
4. Jim, what are you doing? I am doing my homework.
5. Mandy, what are you doing? I am watching television.
6. Tanja, what are you doing? I am reading a book.
7. Julia, what are you doing? I am riding my bike.
8. Peter, what are you doing? I am looking out of the window.
9. Mummy, what are you doing? I am cleaning the window.
10. Maria, what are you doing? I am picking flowers.

17.4 *Seite 83*

1. closing
2. writing
3. smoking
4. playing
5. sitting
6. taking
7. reading
8. cutting
9. swimming
10. making
11. shutting
12. getting
13. eating
14. dancing
15. hiding
16. putting
17. lying

17.5 *Seite 83*

2. are having
3. is writing
4. is swimming
5. is phoning
6. is smoking
7. is running
8. are getting
9. is lying
10. are sitting
11. are closing

17.6 *Seite 84*

2. They are watching TV.
3. She is singing.
4. He is brushing his shoes.
5. The cat is sleeping on the sofa.
6. He is standing on a chair.
7. She is reading a book.
8. The boy is sitting on the table.
9. The children are playing tennis.
10. He is listening to the radio.
11. The boy is singing.
12. He is painting a picture.
13. He is looking at a picture.
14. The girl is writing a letter.
15. He is counting the balls.
16. The boy is playing the saxophone.
17. He is playing the guitar.
18. He is washing the dishes.
19. The boy is playing football.
20. The dog is barking.
21. She is swimming.
22. He is washing the car.
23. She is sitting on a chair.
24. He is reading a letter.

17.7 *Seite 85*

It's (a) quarter to seven. Peter is in bed. He is getting up. He is stretching his arms.
It's half past seven now. Peter is drinking a glass of milk. His sister is eating an apple, his mother is eating cornflakes. His father is reading a newspaper.
It's a quarter past eight. Peter and his sister are standing at the bus stop. They are waiting for the bus.
It's ten to nine. The teacher is standing in front of the class. Peter is reading from a book. The other pupils are sitting on their chairs and are writing in their exercise books.
It's ten to eleven now. Peter is playing football with his friends in the playground. A dog is barking loudly.
It's twenty past four. Peter and his sister are going home. They are getting on a bus. Three boys are coming to the bus stop.
It's six o'clock. Peter is sitting on the floor and watching TV. His father and mother are sitting on the sofa and playing cards. Peter's sister is reading a book.

Seite 86 **17.8**

is coming / is chasing / is cooking / are just going / is still sitting / am doing / is coming / is smiling / is still doing / am taking

Seite 87 **17.9**

are playing / is drawing / are writing / are doing / are looking / are watching / are standing / is coming / is carrying

18. The Auxiliary *can* / Das Hilfsverb „können“

Seite 88 **18.1**

1. sail	5. swim	9. skate
2. ride a bike	6. ride a horse	10. play football
3. dance	7. ski	11. fish
4. play tennis	8. climb trees	12. organise his stamps

Setze nun jeweils das Hilfsverb *can* vor das Verb und bilde Sätze.
He can ride a horse and a bike.
Fred can dance, sail, swim and skate.
He can ski and fish.
Fred can climb trees and organise his stamps.
Fred can play tennis.

Seite 89 **18.2**

Fred can't play the guitar with his broken arm.
He can eat with a spoon.
He can't use his computer.
Fred can't take a shower.
He can't do his homework.
Fred can go to bed.
He can't open bottles.
He can go to school.
He can't wash his ears.
He can't climb trees.

Seite 90 **18.3**

Hier kommt es darauf an inhaltlich sinnvolle Sätze zu bilden, z. B.:
Dogs can bark very loudly but they can't sing.
Budgies can sing very well but they can't smell very well.
Lions can climb trees but they can't sing.
Monkeys can eat bananas but they can't bark.
Horses can pull carts but they can't catch mice.
Snakes can live a long time without water but they can't jump.
Cats can catch mice but they can't fly.
Bears can swim but they can't sing.

Seite 90 **18.4**

B: I'm thinking of an animal.
A: Can it climb trees, Bob?
B: No, it can't.
A: Can it fly?
B: No, it can't.
A: Can it walk on two legs?
B: No, it can't.
A: Can it hear well?
B: Yes, it can.
A: Is it a lion?
B: No, it isn't.
A: Is it a dog?
B: Yes, it is.

18.5 *Seite 91*

Hier sind noch ein paar weitere Beispiele:
I can play football but I can't play an instrument.
I can write good stories but I can't draw clowns.
I can climb trees but I can't catch snakes.

18.6 *Seite 91*

Beantworte die Frage entweder nach der Vorgabe – wenn sie auf dich zutreffen – oder finde eigene Antworten. Zum Beispiel:
Can you go out whenever you want? Yes, I can but I have to ask my parents first.
What time do you have to be home? I have to be at home by seven o'clock.

19. Simple Present Tense / Das einfache Präsens

19.1 *Seite 92*

1. Harry's parents get up at seven o'clock every day.
2. They all have breakfast in the kitchen.
3. He goes to school by bus.
4. They live in the country.
5. Harry's mother is a teacher
6. They come home at four 'o clock.
7. In the afternoon Harry often plays football with his friends.
8. He listens to pop music.
9. He likes pop music.
10. In the evening they watch television.

19.2 *Seite 93*

2. it flies 3. she gets 4. he fetches 5. it does 6. she buys 7. it catches
8. he cooks 9. she hurries 10. he goes 11. she kisses

19.3 *Seite 94*

Halte dich bei Mustafa, Sven und Paula einfach an das Beispiel.

19.4 *Seite 94*

His name is David. He is thirty years old. He comes from Great Britain and lives in London. He lives in a flat which has four rooms. He works in a big school as a teacher. He speaks English and German. He is married and has two children. He likes football, fishing and travelling to Italy. He hates boxing, watching TV, beer and warm milk. In his spare time he plays tennis and he collects stamps and records.

19.5 *Seite 95*

Fred sometimes listens to CDs with friends. He often reads books. Fred often plays football in the school team and he never does housework. He usually watches TV in the evening.
Daniel never listens to CDs on Mondays. He never plays football but sometimes he reads books. He seldom helps with the housework and sometimes he watches pop shows on TV.
Peter listens to CDs every day. He seldom reads books and never plays football. Every day he does housework and he often likes watching action movies on TV.

19.6 *Seite 96*

3. Fred washes the clothes.
4. Fred empties the dustbin.
5. Fred cleans the floor.
6. Fred cleans the shoes.
7. Fred sets the table.
8. Fred washes the dishes.
9. Fred makes the beds.

10. Fred makes breakfast.
11. Fred tidies the room.
12. Fred washes the car.
13. Fred does the shopping.

Seite 96 **19.7**

Denke an deine Familie und überlege, wie häufig du und der Rest der Familie welche Aufgaben im Haushalt erledigen. Zum Beispiel:
I often lay the table and sometimes I do the washing-up. I never repair broken things. My father always repairs broken things and washes the car. He sometimes cleans the shoes. My mother usually does the cooking and she often does the shopping. My brother never does the cooking, the washing-up or the shopping. He never lays the table or cleans the shoes, and he never repairs broken things. He is too small. He is just three years old. But he is nice and I like him very much.

Seite 97 **19.8**

The dog wags its tail. Then the bell rings. The hen lays an egg. The egg falls into a net. After that the gun fires. It makes a hole in the fishtank. Then the water pours down. Finally the sleeping boy wakes up.

Seite 97 **19.9**

Fred stretches his arms. He rubs his eyes and gets out of bed. Then Fred goes into the bathroom. He washes his hands and his face. Then he has a shower. After that he dries his body with a towel. He puts on his shirt and his pants. Then he goes downstairs to the kitchen. There he sits down at the breakfast table and has breakfast. Finally Fred leaves the house and goes to the bus stop.

Seite 98 **19.10**

1. Look! It is beginning to rain.
2. We are having English now.
3. Mr. Evans laughs very much.
4. The bus always stops at this corner.
5. We have English four times a week.
6. It's 8 o'clock. The bus is coming.

Seite 100 **19.12**

1. true	8. false	15. true	22. false
2. false	9. true	16. false	23. true
3. false	10. false	17. false	24. false
4. true	11. false	18. true	25. true
5. false	12. true	19. false	26. true
6. false	13. false	20. false	
7. true	14. true	21. false	

Die Korrekturen der falschen Aussagen lauten:
2. Cinderella has two stepsisters.
3. Her sisters don't help in the house.
5. Cinderella's sisters go to the ball.
6. Cinderella hasn't got any dress or shoes.
8. The prince holds a ball, not the king.
10. The fairy gives Cinderella a wonderful dress.
11. The coach has got six horses.
13. The prince dances with Cinderella.
16. Cinderella loses her shoe.

17. The prince can't see Cinderella.
19. The prince's men go from house to house.
20. Cinderella's stepsisters want to try the shoe on.
21. The shoe fits Cinderella because it is her shoe.
22. The men say to Cinderella, "You are the girl."
24. The prince will marry Cinderella.

19.13 Seite 101

Time (When?)	Place (Where?)	People/Things (Who / What?)	Actions / Events / Facts (What happens?) Reasons (Why?)
at midnight	at the ball	Cinderella prince	dance all night fall in love Cinderella looks beautiful
midnight	at the castle	Cinderella prince	runs away loses one's shoe looks for Cinderella but can't find her
the next morning	at the castle at Cinderella's house	prince men men Cinderella sisters	go from house to house wants to find Cinderella shoe must fit try on shoe shoe doesn't fit puts on shoe, fits It's Cinderella's shoe
	at the castle	men Cinderella prince	takes Cinderella to the castle marries Cinderella are very happy

19.14 Seite 101

Cinderella lives with her evil stepmother and her two evil stepsisters. She is very unhappy because they hate her and she has to work in the house all day. One day the prince holds a ball at his castle. The two sisters go to the ball. Cinderella can't go. She has got no dress and no shoes. Cinderella starts to cry but suddenly a fairy appears. She gives Cinderella a dress and a pair of shoes. A coach with six horses takes her to the castle. But she must be back home by midnight.
Cinderella dances with the prince and they fall in love. But the prince doesn't know who she is. At 12 o'clock Cinderella runs back home and loses a silk shoe. The prince tells his men to look for the girl all over the town. Finally they find Cinderella because the shoe fits. They marry and live happily ever after.

20. Questions and Negations with *to do* / Fragen und Verneinungen mit *to do*

20.1 Seite 102

Lies zuerst den Fragebogen genau durch. Schlage unbekannte Wörter im *dictionary* nach. Kreuze dann die Antworten, die auf dich zutreffen bei *Yes* an. Die anderen erhalten das Kreuz bei *No*. Wenn du alle Fragen beantwortet hast, fertige einen zusammenhängenden Text. Dein Text könnte ungefähr wie folgt lauten:

I live with my parents and I have got one brother. My name is ... and I'm 12 years old. My brother is 14 years old. My parents let me go out with my friends but I have to tell them where I'm going. On Sundays we usually have a big family meal. My father helps with the cooking and my brother and I lay the table and do the washing-up

(We don't have a dishwasher). Sometimes my aunt and uncle come to see us and we all play games. On schooldays I have to do my homework after lunch. I usually spend less then two hours on my homework. We have to help at home. We tidy up our bedrooms, go shopping with our father or mother and clean our bikes.

Seite 104 **20.2**

2. Does he eat bananas? Yes, he does.
3. Does she fly planes? Yes, she does.
4. Does she go to school? Yes, she does.
5. Does he wash the dishes? Yes, he does.

Seite 104 **20.3**

2. Do you speak English?
3. Does Peter ride his bike?
4. Do I know my headmaster?
5. Do you often go to the cinema?
6. Do teachers mark tests?
7. Does the pilot fly planes?
8. Do we play tennis every summer?
9. Do children like sweets?
10. Does she live on the second floor?
11. Does Fred like dogs?

Seite 105 **20.4**

2. Does she go to the bathroom?
3. Does her mother make her breakfast?
4. Do her father and Jimmy come down from the bedroom?
5. Does the dog bark in the garden?
6. Does Jimmy open the door and go into the garden?
7. Do Peter, Brenda and Susan wait at the gate?
8. Do they all go to school?
9. Does it snow in winter?
10. Does Jack remember him?
11. Does he speak English very clearly?
12. Does John laugh a lot?
13. Do we come to class on time?
14. Does your father play football?
15. Do I wash my face every morning?

Seite 106 **20.5**

Hier geht es darum zu sagen, welche Nahrungsmittel du magst und welche nicht. Schlage zuerst die Namen der Nahrungsmittel, die du nicht kennst, in einem *dictionary* nach. Ordne dann die Nahrungsmittel nach Essbarem und Trinkbarem. Schreibe anschließend deine Vorlieben und Abneigungen auf.
Zum Beispiel: I don't like water but I like juice. I like milk but I don't like coffee. I don't like potatoes but I like rice. I like tomatoes but I don't like carrots. I don't like bread but I like cake and chocolate etc.

Seite 107 **20.6**

Mr. Brown likes watching TV but he doesn't like going to work.
Mr. Brown likes cleaning his car but he doesn't like doing the washing-up.
Mr. Brown likes listening to music but he doesn't like reading the newspaper.
Mr. Brown likes going out for walks but he doesn't like driving his car.

20.7 *Seite 108*

Billy: Do you like to go to school?
Brenda: Yes, I do.
Billy: Do you learn English at school?
Brenda: No, I don't.
Brenda: Does your teacher speak German?
Billy: Yes, he does.
Billy: Does your teacher drink milk during the lesson?
Brenda: No, he doesn't.
Brenda: Does your teacher read the newspaper during lesson?
Billy: No, he doesn't.
Billy: Do your parents help you with your homework?
Brenda: Yes, they do.
Billy: Do you and your friends like geography?
Brenda: No, we don't.

20.8 *Seite 108*

Hier sollst du wieder Auskunft über deine Person geben. Beantworte die Fragen bitte jeweils mit *Yes, I do.* oder *No, I don't.* Zum Beispiel:
Do you live with your parents? Yes, I do.
Do you often watch TV? Yes, I do.
Do you like watching football games? No, I don't.
etc.

21. Parts of the Body

21.1 *Seite 109*

1. head	4. ears	7. thumb / hand
2. nose	5. hair	8. eyes
3. mouth	6. toes / foot	

21.2 *Seite 110*

2. chest / head	6. hair	10. hands
3. legs	7. hand	11. eyes
4. tummy	8. nose	12. fingers
5. head	9. ears	

21.3 *Seite 110*

mouth – call / eat / drink / speak / laugh / smile / kiss / talk
ears – sounds / words / music / teacher
hands – write / carry / lift / point / draw
legs and feet – walk / dance / rush / jump / stand / run / hurry

21.4 *Seite 111*

2. hand	8. toe	14. chest
3. foot	9. nose	15. stomach
4. chin	10. mouth	16. hair
5. knee	11. head	17. thumb
6. ear	12. leg	18. eye
7. finger	13. shoulder	19. forehead

21.5 *Seite 111*

2 – 3 – 1

21.6 *Seite 113*

von links nach rechts: Jack, Bill, Ned

Seite 113 **21.7**

Bei dieser Übung sollst du auf Englisch eine oder mehrere der abgebildeten Personen beschreiben ohne den Namen zu nennen. Dein Freund soll raten, welche Person(en) du beschreibst.
Beispiel : Coco
I'm thinking of a person. He is a man. He's got a square face with large ears. His mouth is wide, his lips are thin. He's got short, curly hair and a big straight nose. His eyes are big and round. Can you guess which person I'm thinking of?

Edward:
face: round
ears: small, close to head
nose: big
eyes: small
mouth: narrow,
moustache
head: bald

Nick:
nose: big
eyes: small
mouth: small
ears: small
hair: curly

Jojo:
face: round
hair: fringe
mouth: wide, big teeth
ears: small
nose: short, small
eyes: small, glasses

Aunt Mary:
face: round
ears: big
eyes: small, glasses
nose: short
mouth: small, narrow
hair: straight

Elizabeth:
face: square
eyes: big, round
nose: small
mouth: wide, full lips
hair: curly, long

22. Clothes

Seite 114 **22.1**

Dick is wearing a blue shirt and green trousers.

Seite 115 **22.2**

Fred: shirt, tie, jacket, trousers, socks, shoes
Freda: hat, gloves, pullover, skirt, shoes

Seite 115 **22.3**

3. boots
4. trousers
5. tie
6. socks
7. sandals
8. sweater
9. cardigan
10. blouse
11. shoes
12. jacket

Seite 116 **22.4**

1. trousers
2. boots
3. tracksuit
4. running shoes
5. raincoat
6. sandals
7. umbrella
8. skirt
9. swimming trunks
10. socks
11. shirt
12. gloves
13. cap
14. scarf
15. hat
16. T-shirt
17. waistcoat

Seite 117 **22.5**

a patterned dress
a striped blouse
a striped skirt
a spotted tie
a long-sleeved cardigan
a sleeveless jumper
checked trousers

Seite 118 **22.7**

a green leather jacket
patterned stockings
striped leather shoes
a pair of sunglasses
a black skirt
a ring in her ear

23. Houses and Homes

23.1 *Seite 119*

detached house / flat / cottage / farmhouse / castle / ghost / Eskimo / igloo / dog / kennel

23.2 *Seite 120*

Trage zuerst die Angaben, die auf dich zutreffen, in die Lücken ein. Benutze dann deine Angaben und beschreibe dein Heim.
Zum Beispiel: Today I want to tell you about the block of flats where I live. My home is not far from my school. It is on the second floor. There are six rooms. Our house has got a large garden at the back where children can play. Our flat has got a balcony, too. Sometimes my mother uses it for hanging out the washing. In the summertime we often have our meals on the balcony.

23.3 *Seite 121*

1. He lives in a semi-detached house.
2. There are seven rooms altogether.
3. He is happy because he can watch people from his window and he can play in the loft and in the garden.
4. The first room is the hall.
5. They eat their meals in the living room on Sundays and Peter watches television there and listens to his parents' stereo.
6. They have their meals in the kitchen on weekdays.
7. He can see people passing their house.
8. Yes, there is. It's the loft.
9. The washing machine is in the cellar.
10. Yes, there is a small back garden.

24. The *there*-Structure / Die *there*-Struktur

24.1 *Seite 124*

3. There is a bathtub downstairs in the children's bedroom.
4. There are pigs downstairs in the kitchen.
5. There is a coffee pot hanging from the ceiling.
6. There are clothes hanging on a line in the bedroom.
8. Is there a shower upstairs in the sitting room? Yes, there is.
9. Are there pigs downstairs in the bedroom? No, there aren't.
10. Are there books on the shelf? Yes, there are.
11. Is there a washing machine on the bed? Yes, there is.
12. Is there a TV set downstairs in the kitchen? No, there isn't.
13. Is there a boy sitting downstairs on the chair? No, there isn't.

24.2 *Seite 125*

von oben nach unten:
station / disco / supermarket / playground / swimming pool / bus stop / post office / restaurant

Du musst nur die Wörter für die Gebäude oder Orte entsprechend austauschen.

25. Prepositions / Präpositionen

Seite 127 **25.1**

2. Brian is sitting under the table.
3. Anne is hiding behind the tree.
4. Tony is lying on the roof of the garage.
5. Jenny is hiding behind the house.
6. The dog is sitting under the chair.

Seite 127 **25.2**

2. The elephant is walking in front of the zebra.
3. The zebra is walking between the elephant and the giraffe.
4. The lion is walking behind the clown.
5. The clown is walking behind the horse.
6. The bear is at the end.
7. The camel is walking between the monkey and the horse.
8. The lion is walking in front of the bear.
9. The giraffe is walking between the monkey and the zebra.
10. The horse is walking behind the camel.

Seite 128 **25.3**

4 – 5 – 1 – 6 – 3 – 2

Seite 128 **25.4**

The boy is standing between the trees.
Tony is hiding behind the door.
The oranges are in the box.
The car is waiting in front of the house.
The dog is lying under the car.

Seite 129 **25.5**

along / up / after / over / against / into

Seite 130 **25.6**

2. It is flying into the glass.
3. It is sitting on the table.
4. Now it is going down the table leg.
5. Now it is walking across the floor.
6. It is climbing up the wall.
7. Now it is flying over the bookshelf.
8. It is climbing up the curtain.
9. At last it is flying out of the window.

Seite 131 **25.7**

Let's talk about the picture. It is a circus. Can you see the big elephant? It is walking into the circus ring. Try to find the horse which is running out of it. A clown is sitting in a car. Another clown is falling out. There are three boys in the circus. They are riding bikes. One of them rides in front, one behind and one is between them. Can you see the clown with the dog? The dog is running to the clown. Can you see the two men flying through the air? Two others are going up and down. Two girls are standing on their horses. They are riding round a man. One clown is not in the circus ring. He is sitting with his back against the wall.

Register

f. bedeutet: Du findest das Stichwort auf dieser und auf der folgenden Seite.
ff. bedeutet: Du findest das Stichwort auf dieser und auf mehreren folgenden Seiten.

Was haben dieser Elefant und diese Schüler gemeinsam?*
*Das Gelernte ist im Langzeitgedächtnis
Deutsch: sehr gut
Englisch: sehr gut
Mathe: sehr gut
8. Klasse
Mit Download für
phase-6
mentor
- Coole Lernhilfe mit Download
- Mit phase-6 einfach ins Langzeitgedächtnis
- ein Fach, eine Klasse, ein Band
Ein Fach, eine Klasse, ein Band - inklusive elektronischer Karteikärtchen für phase-6 zum Downloaden. So kannst du den Schulstoff wirklich verstehen und garantiert behalten. Gibt's jeweils für die 5. bis 8. Klasse.
Weitere Infos unter www.mentor.de/sehrgut
mentor
Eine Klasse besser.